W9-AAZ-257

‹ AUSTRALIA ›

AUSTRALIA

Laura Dolce

CHELSEA HOUSE PUBLISHERS
Philadelphia

Chelsea House Publishers

Contributing Author: Derek Davis

3   5   7   9   8   6   4   2

Library of Congress Cataloging-in-Publication Data

Dolce, Laura.
Australia / Laura Dolce.
p.   cm. — (Major world nations)
Includes index.
Summary: An introduction to the geography, history, government,
economy, people, and culture of the "land down under."
ISBN 0–7910–4731–8 (hardcover)
1. Australia—Juvenile literature.   [1. Australia.]
I. Title.   II. Series.
DU96.D65   1997
994—dc21   97–23404
CIP
AC

◂CONTENTS▸

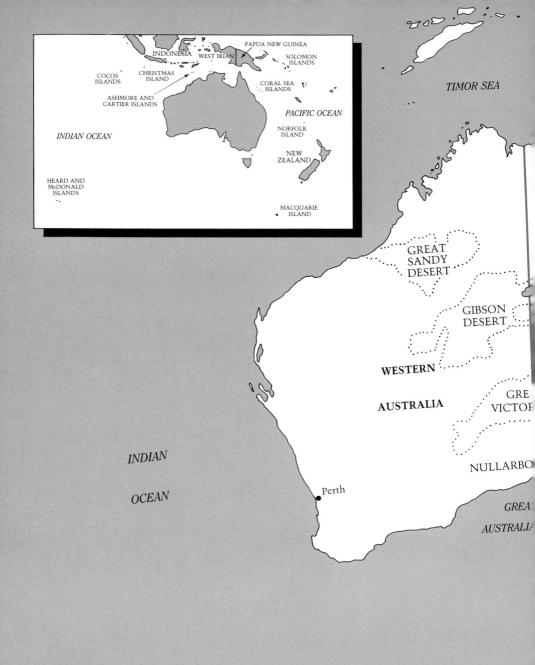

INDONESIA   WEST IRIAN   PAPUA NEW GUINEA

COCOS
ISLANDS

CHRISTMAS
ISLAND

ASHMORE AND
CARTIER ISLANDS

CORAL SEA
ISLANDS

SOLOMON
ISLANDS

PACIFIC OCEAN

INDIAN OCEAN

NORFOLK
ISLAND

NEW
ZEALAND

HEARD AND
McDONALD
ISLANDS

MACQUARIE
ISLAND

TIMOR SEA

GREAT
SANDY
DESERT

GIBSON
DESERT

WESTERN

AUSTRALIA

GRE
VICTOR

NULLARBO

INDIAN

OCEAN

Perth

GREA

AUSTRALIA

◄ FACTS AT A GLANCE ►

Land and People

Area	2,966,151 square miles (7,682,300 square kilometers)
Highest Point	Mount Kosciusko, 7,310 feet (2,228 meters)
Major River System	The Murray-Darling
Capital	Canberra (population 300,000)
Population	Over 18 million
Population Distribution	Urban, 85 percent; rural, 15 percent
Official Language	English
Literacy Rate	98.5 percent
Religions	Anglicanism, 26 percent; Catholicism, 26 percent; other Christian, 24 percent
Holidays	New Year's Day, January 1; ANZAC Day, April 25; Christmas, December 25

Economy

Chief Exports	Machinery, ores and scrap metal, coal, gold, meat, wool, wheat
Chief Imports	Machinery, transport equipment, chemicals
Industry	Food processing, machinery, steel, automobiles, aircraft, ships, chemicals, refined petroleum, fertilizers, plastics, pharmaceuticals, textiles, service industries

Employment	Commerce and services, 70 percent of the work force; manufacturing, 14 percent; construction, 7 percent; agriculture, 5 percent; government and public works, 5 percent

Government

Form of Government	Federated parliamentary state with House of Representatives and Senate; state or territorial governments
Head of Government	Prime minister, leader of the majority party
Formal Head of State	Queen of England, represented by governor-general
Cabinet	Appointed by prime minister from his party
Political Parties	National Country party, Labor party
Voting Rights	All citizens over 18 years of age must vote

◄HISTORY AT A GLANCE►

1788	Captain Arthur Phillip and the First Fleet land at Botany Bay.
1790	The Second Fleet arrives.
1813	Explorers find a way through the Blue Mountains. Settlement of the interior begins.
1829	Britain lays claim to the entire continent.
1835	Melbourne is founded by John Pascoe Fawkner and John Batman.
1851	Gold is discovered in Victoria and New South Wales. Victoria separates from New South Wales.
1859	Queensland separates from New South Wales.
1872	The first international telegraph line is completed from Port Darwin to Banjoewanji, Indonesia.
1898	The federal constitution is written.
1901	Australia is declared an independent commonwealth.
1909	The Australian navy is created.
1911	The Northern Territory is formed. Canberra cedes from New South Wales to become the Australian Capital Territory.
1914	Australia enters World War I.
1915	More than 8,000 Australian soldiers are lost in the battle at Gallipoli.

1939   Australia enters World War II.

1945   The National Airlines Act establishes Trans-Australia Airlines.

1962   Australia sends 30 advisers to Vietnam.

1965   Australian troops are sent to Vietnam.

1966   The United States requests and receives additional troop support from Australia in Vietnam.

1972   Australia pulls out of Vietnam.

1973   The Sydney Opera House is completed.

1983   The *Australia II* wins the America's Cup.

1988   Australia celebrates its bicentennial.

1990   Aboriginal and Torres Strait Islanders Commission established to give indigenous peoples greater voice in government programs that affect them.

1993   Native Title Act passed to help aborigines press land claims.

‹ AUSTRALIA ›

Australians stroll through a plaza in downtown Brisbane, the capital of Queensland. Many of Australia's cities are noted for their large open spaces and public parks that allow residents to enjoy Australia's sunny weather.

Australia and the World

On January 18, 1788, six British ships under the command of Captain Arthur Phillip dropped anchor in a bay on a mainly unexplored land mass in the Southern Hemisphere—Australia. Their arrival heralded the birth of a new nation and the exploration of a continent. Huddled in the bowels of the ships were 772 terrified convicts—568 men, 191 women, and 13 children—all prisoners who had been transported from British jails to this vast, arid land to serve out their sentences. These people were the first European settlers in Australia.

Two centuries later, the nation of Australia celebrated its bicentennial—the 200th anniversary of the arrival of the British convict ships. Like the United States and Canada, Australia was first colonized by British settlers. As in the United States and Canada, these Europeans displaced a native population that had occupied a continent for thousands of years. And like the United States and Canada, Australia is now a powerful, industrialized nation with a high standard of living. But although the three countries are similar in many ways, Australia's unique geography and unusual history have made it very different from its North American counterparts.

Australia is the only nation to occupy an entire continent, although its area of 2,966,151 square miles (7,682,300 square kilometers) makes it the smallest of the world's 7 continents. Surrounded by the South Pacific and Indian oceans, Australia is also an island. Its area is almost equal to that of the continental United States, but the population of the United States is 15 times greater than Australia's population of slightly more than 18 million.

The island-continent abounds in animals and plants that exist nowhere else. Kangaroos, koalas, duck-billed platypuses, eucalyptus trees, and emus live in Australia, which is the driest inhabited continent on earth. (Antarctica is drier, but it is considered uninhabited.) Semidesert plains and inhospitable deserts cover 70 percent of its area, so over 80 percent of Australians live in cities, most of which are on the coast, where more rain falls. A few of Australia's original inhabitants, the aborigines, live in the barren, mostly flat interior called the outback.

The aborigines lived in Australia long before any Europeans visited the continent. They were a nomadic people—that is, they traveled throughout the land in search of animals to hunt and plants to gather for food. Because they depended on nature in order to live, they regarded the natural world with great respect. According to the aborigines, humans are part of nature and nature is part of humans, all created by spirits who still exist and inhabit their creation. The aborigines' complex system of spiritual beliefs involved all they saw around them. But the early European colonists thought that the aborigines lived like animals and possessed little intelligence because they did not build houses, wear much clothing, or cultivate crops. Consequently, they treated the aborigines even less humanely than European settlers in North and South America treated Native Americans.

Although the arrival of the First Fleet, as the original convict ships came to be called, marked the beginning of British colonization, the British were not the first Europeans to reach the continent. In the 17th century, traders from Holland were active in the East

Indies (the area of present-day Java, Sumatra, and Papua New Guinea, islands in the Indian Ocean and the South Pacific Ocean). In 1606 a Dutch ship commanded by Willem Jansz made the first landing by Europeans on Australian soil when it reached the Cape York Peninsula, 90 miles (144 kilometers) south of Papua New Guinea. Dutch sailors then went on to map almost half of the Australian coast. They named the continent New Holland. Abel Tasman, the greatest of the Dutch navigators, discovered the neighboring islands of Tasmania, New Zealand, and Fiji in 1642–43. Traders soon lost interest in New Holland, however, because it seemed barren, offered little of commercial value, and was peopled by the aborigines, whom the Dutch called "savages."

In 1768, the British government, the British navy, and the Royal Society (a respected group of scientists) planned an expedition to explore the South Pacific. Led by Captain James Cook, a skilled navigator, the expedition visited the eastern shore of New Holland in 1770. Captain Cook visited a place he named Botany Bay for the large number of botanic specimens (plant life) he found there, and he brought back glowing reports of rich, brown soil suitable for farming.

Captain James Cook (1728–79) explored much of the South Pacific for his British sponsors. His excellent map and less than accurate description of Australia's eastern coast inspired the British government to establish the first European settlement there.

In 1776, Great Britain's North American colonies declared their independence. This event shaped Australia's future. The British government had been getting rid of large numbers of convicted criminals by sending them to North America, but the revolutionary war put an end to that program. Encouraged by Captain Cook's reports on Australia, Great Britain decided that this new continent was the answer to its overcrowded prisons. Those who arrived on the First Fleet at Botany Bay, however, soon discovered that the rich farmlands described by Cook were an illusion. Instead, the weary travelers were surrounded by mile after mile of sandy wilderness. Within a few days the fleet was forced to move to nearby Port Jackson harbor (later renamed Sydney). It was here that the first colony was founded. Soon more prison ships arrived and more colonies were formed. In the years that followed still more ships arrived, filled with British citizens looking for a fresh start in life. As the colonies grew, so did British control, until in 1829 Britain laid claim to the entire continent.

Throughout the 1800s colonists, explorers, and settlers spread across the continent. Sheep and cattle ranching, the discovery of gold in the 1850s, better methods of growing wheat, and expanding immigration all contributed to Australia's spectacular growth in the 19th century. By 1859 six colonies had been established, and Australians began to realize that a more efficient government could be created if all the colonies worked together in a federation. After negotiations between the colonies, a constitution was written, and in 1901 the former colonies became an independent nation in the British Commonwealth. Australia's transition from a cluster of colonies to an independent and united nation was peaceful, unlike that of the United States.

In the 20th century, Australia is a highly industrialized nation, known as one of the many countries where large numbers of men and women received a chance at a new beginning. Australia deserves this reputation, having welcomed to its shores nearly 5 million immigrants, over one-fourth of the 18 million people currently living there. Australia has absorbed people of many diverse cultures and backgrounds into its population. The plight of the aborigines, however, has marred Australia's reputation in the eyes of the rest of the world.

Today, the aborigines live on reservations or in city slums. Many of them are unemployed, lack good health care, and exist in squalid living conditions. Amid the pageantry of the bicentennial celebration there were echoes of anger over the way aborigines have been treated. Since the 1970s, a succession of Land Rights Acts has returned large tracts of unproductive land and some sacred areas to aboriginal control, but many civil rights issues remain unresolved.

Australia's coat of arms features the kangaroo and the emu, two of the unusual animals that are found only on the island-continent.

Although abundantly supplied with natural resources, Australia is the driest of the inhabited continents. Waterfalls such as Twin Falls, in Kakadu National Park, are an uncommon but welcome sight.

Other problems facing Australia are economic. Australia is rich in natural assets, with abundant natural gas and oil supplies, a wealth of minerals, thousands of acres of pasture for sheep and cattle, and fertile regions for raising wheat and other crops. After World War II, manufacturing and mining industries boomed, aided by government policies. The nation produces so much that it usually exports more than it imports. But in the 1970s and 1980s Asian nations expanded their economies as well, and Australia struggled to keep up. Prices rose, and more and more Australians found it difficult to get jobs. A severe recession struck the country in 1990–91, but economic growth rebounded over the next few years, the national budget deficit was reduced, and unemployment returned to close to 8 percent of the workforce. Today, despite strong trade agreements with the United States and other countries, Australia is scrambling to hold its own on the export market, where the goods it produces compete against those from Taiwan, Japan, the People's Republic of China, and South Korea.

Because Australia was settled and populated by Europeans and their descendants, it has traditionally been tied to Europe, particularly to Great Britain. Yet Europe is on the other side of the globe. In the second half of the 20th century the nearby Asian nations have become increasingly important players on the world stage. Out of necessity, Australia has begun a shift in foreign policy and trade focus from Europe to Asia, including tariff reduction and promotion of an Asia-Pacific free trade area by the year 2020.

In addition, Australia is a comparatively young nation and in some ways is still feeling the growing pains caused by its transition from wild frontier to industrialized nation. It appears that Australia must reconcile many conflicting facets of its national identity: rugged outback individualism, traditional British heritage, and native aborigine culture. And to maintain a strong, independent position in global affairs Australia must meet the challenge of Asian domination of the Pacific area. These are daunting tasks, yet in this unique land of the eucalyptus tree and the koala, where the first convict settlers scratched an existence out of a harsh land and went on to build a nation, anything is possible.

Ayers Rock, an enormous sandstone boulder in the Northern Territory, is both a sacred site to the aborigines and a national park that attracts tourists from all over the world.

The Land Down Under

The island-continent of Australia lies southeast of the Asian land mass, with the Indian Ocean washing its western and southern shores. On the north, Australia is bordered by the Timor Sea and the Arafura Sea; beyond these seas lie the islands of Indonesia and Papua New Guinea, Australia's closest neighbors. On the east, the Coral Sea separates Australia from the island chain called the Solomon Islands, and the Tasman Sea separates it from New Zealand, its neighbor to the southeast. Beyond the Solomons and New Zealand is the vast Pacific Ocean.

Although it is the newest continent in historical terms, having been settled by Europeans only a few hundred years ago, Australia is the oldest in geological terms. In 1983, scientists determined that grains of rock from Western Australia were 4.1 billion to 4.2 billion years old—the oldest ever found on the planet.

Australia is primarily a flat continent. Only 5 percent of it is more than 2,000 feet (600 meters) above sea level; the average height is less than 1,000 feet (300 meters) above sea level. From east to west, the island has four main geographic regions. They are the eastern lowland plain, the eastern highlands, the central plains, and the western plateau.

The eastern lowland plain is a narrow strip of level land along the eastern ocean shore from Cape York Peninsula in the north to the city of Melbourne in the south. Much of the northern half of this plain is forested. A few miles offshore is the Great Barrier Reef, which runs for 1,200 miles (1,900 kilometers) along the coast. It is the largest coral reef in the world and is a paradise for both tropical sea life and scuba divers. The southern part of the plain is the site of many of Australia's cities and towns, including Brisbane, Sydney, Canberra (the country's capital), and Melbourne. This region also has Australia's most fertile soil and many flourishing farms.

At the western edge of the narrow plain is the eastern highlands, a ridge of hills and mountains that separates the lowland from the interior of the continent. In the north, this barrier is called the Eastern Highlands or the Great Dividing Range. In the south, the highlands barrier consists of the Blue Mountains, west of Sydney, and the Australian Alps, in the southeast corner of the country. The mountains are between 1,000 and 7,000 feet (300 and 2,100 meters) high. The highest point in Australia, the peak of Mount Kosciusko in the Australian Alps, is 7,310 feet (2,228 meters) above sea level.

West of the highlands is Australia's third geographic region, the central plains. This is a region of large, low-lying, dry depressions called basins. One of them, in the east-central part of the country, is called the Great Artesian Basin. With an area of 676,250 square miles (1,751,480 square kilometers), it is the largest inland drainage area in the world. Lake Eyre, at the southern edge of this basin, is the continent's lowest point, 39 feet (12 meters) below sea level. The central plains region is crossed by several ranges of low, eroded mountains, including the Macdonnell, James, and Musgrave ranges.

The western plateau covers the western half of the continent. Its rocky or sandy ridges and plains are 1,000 to 2,000 feet (300 to 600 meters) above sea level. Australia's large and forbidding des-erts—the Great Sandy, the Gibson, the Great Victoria, and the Tan-

*Loaded with gear, a rugged vehicle
sets forth along a rutted outback road.*

ami—are found here. In the north, jungle and swamp cover the area known as Arnhem Land on the shore of a large bay called the Gulf of Carpentaria. In the south, the level Nullarbor Plain borders another large bay called the Great Australian Bight.

Australia has many rivers, but nearly all of them run only during the wettest two or three months of the year, at which time they often flood. The rest of the time, they are dry. The only year-round rivers are those that make up the Murray-Darling river system in the southeast. The Murray River is Australia's longest, flowing 1,600 miles (2,600 kilometers) from its source in the Australian Alps to its mouth near the city of Adelaide.

Climate and Weather

Because Australia lies in the Southern Hemisphere, on the opposite side of the equator from Europe and North America, it has been called "the land down under" (Australians sometimes say, "the wonder down under"). Its position "below" the equator also gives Australia seasons that are the opposite of those in the north: July is the middle of winter, and January is the peak of summer.

Most of Australia is warm and dry. The southern part of the country is the most comfortable, with temperatures in Melbourne ranging from an average of 48° Fahrenheit (9° Centigrade) in July to 68° F (20° C) in January. Temperatures in the north are much higher; Darwin averages 77° F (25° C) in July and 86° F (30° C) in January. The interior of the continent is the hottest of all. Temperatures there often reach 100° F (38° C) and can go as high as 115° F (46° C).

Rainfall is greatest in the northeast, where an average yearly precipitation of 59 inches (147 centimeters) nourishes tropical rain forests. Tasmania, Victoria, and parts of New South Wales receive more than 30 inches (76 centimeters) of rain each year. About 40 percent of the continent—mostly in the interior—is desert, with an annual rainfall of less than 10 inches (25 centimeters) and dry seasons lasting 8 months or longer. Around these dry, or arid, regions are semiarid zones where enough rain falls to support grass. Many sheep and cattle ranches are found in the semiarid zones, but rainfall is undependable, and prolonged droughts can mean financial tragedy for ranchers. A drought that began in 1979 and continued through the early 1980s brought dust storms, fires, and billions of dollars in crop and livestock losses to central and western Australia.

Winter snow falls on the highest peaks of the Australian Alps, permitting skiing and other winter sports, but Australia has no year-round snow or glaciers. It does, however, have frequent high winds

Cyclone Tracy struck Darwin on Christmas Day, 1974, and destroyed 95 percent of the city, including these homes.

and cyclones around its coasts. One of the worst storms in the island's history occurred on December 25, 1974, when a cyclone and a flood together destroyed the city of Darwin, leaving 20,000 people homeless; the city has since been rebuilt.

Animal and Plant Oddities

Much of the fascination that Australia holds for the rest of the world is due to its unusual plants and animals, many of which are endemic to Australia—that is, they are found nowhere else. Australia has about 400 species of mammals, 200 of lizards, and 700 of birds. Scientists believe that Australia was once connected to the other continents but became separated from them by the sea about 50 million years ago. As a result, plants and animals that have become extinct elsewhere in the world, or that never developed in other continents, are alive today in Australia. Some of these species are considered "living fossils" by biologists.

One such creature is the platypus, which is thought by scientists to be the only surviving representative of the long-ago evolution from reptiles to mammals. The platypus lays eggs like a bird or a reptile, yet it is warm-blooded and nurses its young like a mammal. About the size of muskrats, platypuses are active at dawn and dusk, when they search stream beds for food with their ducklike bills.

The echidna, or spiny anteater, also combines features of the reptiles and the mammals. The female lays one egg at a time and carries it in a fold of her skin until it hatches; she then nurses the young echidna with milk. Echidnas literally scratch a living from the soil with their powerful front claws, which are used to dig up ants and termites.

Koalas, the cute and cuddly Australian "bears" that appear in advertisements for Qantas Airways, are not really bears at all. They are marsupials, members of a class of mammals who carry their young in pouches. Until the 1930s, koalas were hunted for their soft

Furry, tree-dwelling koalas resemble children's teddy bears but are not members of the bear family. Instead, they are marsupials and are found only in Australia.

fur. Today they are protected by law and are one of the most popular sights on Australia's wildlife preserves.

Two of the country's most distinctive animals appear on its coat of arms. One is the emu, a large, flightless bird similar to the ostrich. The other is the kangaroo, a marsupial noted for its ability to run and jump on its powerfully built hind legs. The largest of the many kangaroo species can stand 8 feet (2.5 meters) tall, can jump 27 feet (8 meters), and can run at speeds of 25 miles (40 kilometers) an hour.

Other marsupial species are the bandicoots, the wallabies, the tree kangaroos, and the opossums. Australia's animal life also includes wombats (burrowers similar to wolverines or badgers), dingoes (bushy-tailed wild dogs), Tasmanian devils (small but extremely fierce predatory mammals), and flying foxes (fruit bats).

Australia's bird species include the anhinga, the bellbird, the black swan, the cassowary, the kookaburra (whose braying call has earned it the nickname "laughing jackass"), the lyrebird, the fairy penguin, and many species of parrots and cockatoos, some of which have become popular around the world as pets. Australia's crocodiles, made famous by the movie *Crocodile Dundee*, are found throughout the coastal areas, but the largest are in the northeast. The seas around the island teem with thousands of species of plants, fish, and animals, but the best known of these is probably the great white shark, which cruises the cold offshore currents.

In addition to its endemic species, Australia has many types of plants and animals that have been introduced by settlers. These include buffalo, donkeys, horses, and even camels; herds of these animals now live in the remote semiarid areas. A much smaller (but more troublesome) nonnative animal is the rabbit, which destroys pastureland that could be used for sheep. So numerous and destructive did rabbits become in the late 19th century that in 1907 a 1,000-mile-long (1,600-kilometer-long) fence was built to keep them out

Large, jumping kangaroos are often seen bounding across Australia's plains, but this smaller, shyer tree kangaroo is a member of the same family of species.

of Western Australia. In the 20th century, rabbits have been shot and poisoned by the millions, but they remain Australia's number one animal pest.

Although much of it is barren and dry, Australia does have many varieties of plant life, especially in the coastal and tropical regions — for example, there are 500 species of eucalyptus trees. These trees are the preferred home of the koalas, which feed on their leaves; in addition, the leaves of many species have medicinal properties. There are 600 species of acacia trees (a spindly tree with fine, feathery leaves) and 470 varieties of orchids, many of which are prized by flower lovers all over the world for their gorgeous colors. Other common trees are the baobab, red cedar, blackwood, jarrah, Queensland maple, and silky oak. Some native species shed their bark each year instead of their leaves.

Like many other nations around the world, Australia is concerned about protecting its wildlife and its environment. More than 30 endangered species are protected by law; these include the banded anteater, the northern hairy-nosed wombat, and the estuarine crocodile. Australia was the first country to pass a law that banned the killing of whales and dolphins. One of Australia's most pressing en-

This baby emu belongs to the world's second largest bird species (only ostriches are larger). The emu feeds on fruits and roots, lives in open grasslands, and cannot fly.

Screw palm trees are among the many species of plant life found in the tropical forests of the Northern Territory.

vironmental issues, however, concerns water: In this driest of continents, water is scarce and often of poor quality, and laws preventing water pollution or wastage are strictly enforced.

States, Cities, and Territories

Australia consists of six states and a number of territories. From largest to smallest, the states are Western Australia, Queensland, South Australia, New South Wales, Victoria, and Tasmania. The largest territory is the Northern Territory, located on the mainland of the continent. Also on the mainland is the Capital Territory, a 900-square-mile (2,400-square-kilometer) area within New South Wales that contains the nation's capital, Canberra. In addition, Australian territory includes a number of small islands in the surrounding seas.

Of the six states, New South Wales is the oldest, and its capital, Sydney, is Australia's oldest city. Located in the southeastern corner of the island, Sydney has a busy international airport and the country's busiest and largest harbor. Most visitors to Australia arrive on the island at Sydney. Of the 6 million people who live in New South Wales, almost 4 million live in Sydney. The city runs down to the harbor, with suburbs spiraling out from it. Although it boasts hundreds of fine restaurants, shops, and businesses, Sydney also exhibits the dark side of modern urban life — the city's King's Crossing district is the haunt of drug pushers, junkies, and prostitutes.

On a more pleasant note, Sydney also has many beautiful beaches — although they are often plagued by sharks. These beaches are carefully watched over by specially trained lifeguards who sound the alarm when a shark's fin is sighted. It is considered a great honor and responsibility to be a lifeguard in Australia, and there is much competition and rivalry among the lifeguards of different beach clubs.

New South Wales is also the site of the Snowy Mountain Hydro Electric Scheme. This large dam took 25 years to build and supplies electricity for southeast Australia as well as irrigation water for 3 states. The most amazing thing about the dam is that it sends water in different directions — sometimes against the flow of gravity — through a complex network of canals, streams, and smaller dams. The Snowy Mountains are Australia's largest winter sports area, and skiing is popular. Not far away is Kosciusko National Park, which surrounds Australia's highest peak with more than 1 million acres of mountain scenery.

The island's largest river system, the Murray-Darling, runs through New South Wales and South Australia. Although small by comparison with the Nile or Mississippi rivers, the Murray-Darling system is large by Australian standards. At one time it was the major route for interstate commerce, but now it is used only for irrigation

At Falls Creek in Victoria, skiers take advantage of the winter snows. This scene is uncharacteristic of most of Australia, which is hot and dry.

and pleasure boating. The Murray provides water for three-fourths of Australia's irrigated cropland.

Located within New South Wales, the Australian Capital Territory is actually a separate district, like the District of Columbia in the United States. The Capital Territory, also called Canberra, houses the center of the federal government, including a new Parliament House on Capitol Hill. Also found in Canberra are the Australian War Memorial, the National Library, and the National Gallery, which houses an art collection.

The state of Victoria is located just south of New South Wales, in the southeastern corner of the country. Its capital city is Melbourne, known for its fine examples of 19th-century architecture and for its conservative, quiet, even old-fashioned way of life.

Queensland is the state in the northeastern corner of the continent, just north of New South Wales. Queensland calls itself "the sunshine state" and relies on tourism for its growing economy. The state has miles of lovely beaches, including one called the Gold Coast—perhaps the best beach in Australia. Queensland also has a rain forest that runs right down to the seacoast and is home to many of the country's unusual animal and bird species.

Another Queensland attraction like none other in the world is the Great Barrier Reef, the world's largest living organism. It is made up of countless trillions of tiny creatures called coral polyps, as well as the skeletons of the many more polyps that have lived and died on the reef over thousands of years. About 250 small islands dot the surface of the reef. A few of them are made entirely of coral (the skeletons of dead polyps) and are called coral cays. The rest of the islands are the tips of mountains that stick up from the sea bottom. Some of them are national parks; others have resorts for scuba divers. The lagoons, or shallow waters between the reef and the shore, are some of the world's best scuba sites because of the more than 1,400 species of tropical fish that live there.

The Northern Territory most closely resembles the typical popular image of Australia. Here, in the outback, sheep stations abound. The aborigines are at home. Termite hills in the Northern Territory stand as tall as men. Stretches of the area are still untouched by human feet. The region is drenched in torrential rains each summer, but for the rest of the year there is no moisture at all. The land is parched and baked by high temperatures for months at a time.

Darwin, the capital, has a population of 80,000 — out of a total population in the territory of only 180,000. Darwin also has a racial mix not found in other Australian cities: One-quarter of its citizens are aborigines, and there is a large Chinese population. In fact, 25 percent of the city's residents were born outside Australia. The other major city in the Northern Territory is Alice Springs, home of the Royal Flying Doctor Service and the School of the Air—services for outback dwellers.

South Australia, just south of the Northern Territory, is home to 1.5 million Australians; over 70 percent of them live in the capital city, Adelaide. Known for its many churches, Adelaide is a beautiful city with something of a small-town atmosphere. Although cooler than the Northern Territory, South Australia has stretches of hot, dry outback. However, it receives some snow in the winter and has several ski resorts.

Western Australia, the largest state, occupies about one-third of the continent. It is cut off from the rest of Australia by deserts — the Nullarbor Plain and the Great Victoria Desert in the south, the Gibson Desert in the middle, and the Great Sandy Desert in the north. More than two-thirds of the state's inhabitants live in the capital city, Perth.

Despite its isolation on Australia's west coast, Perth receives about 1 million tourists each year. The city has grown enormously during the second half of the 20th century, owing to discoveries of mineral deposits in the west. Fortunes made from these discoveries and the businesses they have spawned have given Perth new glitter and polish. Now Perth's high rises and luxury hotels tower over the nearby Swan River and the Indian Ocean shore.

The island-state of Tasmania is separated from the southeastern coast by a narrow sea passage called the Bass Strait. Tasmania, like New South Wales, started out as a penal colony. Hobart, its capital, is the second-oldest city in Australia. Tasmania is hilly and cooler than mainland Australia; at one time it was heavily forested, and some stretches of its original lush forest remain.

Australia claims a number of territories outside the continent and Tasmania. One of them is a large tract in Antarctica, where three scientific research stations are operated by Australians. The others are small islands. The four tiny, uninhabited Ashmore and Cartier Islands are coral reefs in the Indian Ocean that have belonged to Australia since 1934. Christmas Island, northwest of Perth, sup-

Storm Bay lies between Hobart, the capital of Tasmania, and Port Arthur to the southeast. Rocky cliffs, pounded by the ocean, line the bay.

ports a population of several thousand laborers, mostly Chinese and Malaysian, who work in a phosphate mine there; it has belonged to Australia since 1958. The 27 Cocos Islands (formerly called the Keeling Islands), also northwest of Perth, have a population of several hundred people, descendants of servants who once belonged to the island's English owners. The islands have been Australian territory since 1955 and produce small amounts of dried coconut and coconut oil. The Coral Sea Island Territory consists of tiny, uninhabited islets spread over a wide area of the sea off the northeast coast. Heard

Island, southwest of Perth, is a good-sized but bleak island that is actually the peak of a dormant volcano called Big Ben. Nearby to the west are the small McDonald Islands. All of these islands have belonged to Australia since 1947. Macquarie Island, southeast of Hobart, is a small glacier-covered rock that is thought to be one of the largest penguin-breeding colonies in the world. The island has been a dependency of Tasmania since the 19th century. Finally, Norfolk Island, east of Sydney, is the once-notorious prison colony. In 1856, it was settled by descendants of the sailors who mutinied against Captain William Bligh in the famous *Bounty* mutiny of 1789. Today, the families of the mutineers make up about one-quarter of the island's population of 2,000. Farming is productive on this fertile island, but tourism is its main source of income.

Approximately 300,000 aborigines were living in Australia when the first European colonists arrived in 1788; 200 years later, there were around 200,000. Disease and warfare with settlers reduced their numbers drastically, but the aborigine population began to grow in the second half of the 20th century.

A Continent Becomes a Nation

Anthropologists (scientists who study human culture and ways of life) believe that the first aborigines arrived in Australia more than 40,000 years ago, when the level of the ocean was lower and land bridges connected the continents. The aborigines probably walked south from Asia over these bridges. They hunted wild animals, gathered plants for food, and lived and traveled in groups of relatives. They set up communities along shores and rivers near the coast, or farther inland around lakes and streams, where animals came to drink and plant life was plentiful. In spite of this fairly steady food supply, however, frequent droughts, changing weather, and seasonal migrations of animals forced the aborigines to be nomadic, traveling from one water supply to another. They came to know every nuance of the land through their wanderings.

The aborigines also developed spiritual beliefs revolving around the idea of the "Dreamtime," a complicated set of legends that tell of the beginning of earth and man. According to these Dreamtime stories, the world was once flat and barren. Out of this flatness rose the ancestral spirits, who took the shapes of different native animals, plants, and men. Through their many adventures, these spirits created the mountains, rivers, stars, moon, and all living things as well.

When their work was done, the creative part of the Dreamtime came to an end, but Dreamtime itself did not, because the spirits flew into the earth, or the sky, or into different caves and other land formations, where they remain. These places were sacred sites, to be visited only by those who were initiated in special ceremonies in which they were taught to communicate with the spirits in the landscape. These beliefs have shaped the laws and customs of the modern aborigines, who remain a very spiritual people.

In the early 1600s, Europeans began to appear in Australia. The Dutch explorers and navigators did not bother to learn about the aborigine way of life and never settled the land, but even the British, who did colonize Australia in the late 1700s, were not very interested in the natives and their culture and regarded them as uncivilized.

Along with the 772 convicts of the First Fleet, 294 officers arrived in New South Wales to build a settlement. They were dismayed to discover that much of the land was unsuitable for farming. Although a few of the men had some knowledge of agriculture, what little they did know was best applied to English soil and failed dismally when tried in Australia. There appeared to be little water to irrigate this arid new land, and their small herd of livestock did not produce enough manure to fertilize the soil. The settlers started with a bull, a cow, 4 calves, 4 horses, 3 colts, 44 sheep, and several pigs and chickens. But with little food and with only what Captain Arthur Phillip called "rank grass" to graze on, a single sheep was all that remained six months later.

Other problems bedeviled the settlers. Their few tools were badly made and of little help in building shelters or workshops. The settlers themselves were not well suited to wilderness life. Although many of their descendants claimed that the original convicts had been deported for minor crimes such as poaching or for political reasons, they were mostly petty thieves and pickpockets from the streets of London and other cities. They were unused to the rigors of farming and, being used to lives of idleness and crime, were disinclined to work.

At the end of the first six months the lack of nourishing food and adequate clothing had taken its toll. Seventy-eight convicts had died, and many more were sick and unable to work (older people, women, and very young children were not required to do any hard labor). Seeing the morale of the settlers sink lower as the death toll climbed higher, Captain Phillip wrote to the government in London, telling of their troubles and begging for more supplies. In September 1789 the ship *Guardian* left England for Sydney, loaded with provisions for the settlers. Tragically, the ship was wrecked off the coast of Africa and never reached its destination. But the settlers had even

Captain Arthur Phillip (center) brought the convict settlers of the First Fleet to Botany Bay in 1788, founded Sydney, and governed the colony of New South Wales until his return to England in 1792. He was governor during four of the most difficult years of Australia's history.

more troubles in store for them. In 1790 a second fleet arrived, packed with more than 700 convicts—more hungry mouths to fill. For the next two years, the settlers struggled to survive on meager rations. Many, however, succumbed to illness and disease.

By 1792 things had begun to look up. As they became more familiar with the land, the colonists were more successful at raising grains and vegetables. A new public farming program was established and worked well. In this program, groups of convicts worked pieces of land, producing stores of food for public consumption instead of each household working its own land for its own use. In this way, no one starved. The settlement began to expand. Some colonists moved to the more fertile land of Rose Hill, 15 miles (24 kilometers) from Sydney. This expansion was partly due to the freeing of convicts. Realizing that the convicts would work harder if they were working toward a goal, Captain Phillip allowed them to work off their sentences. Former convicts were known as emancipists. Each was given a tract of land to work on his or her own.

British settlement of Australia also expanded when penal colonies were established on Norfolk Island, an islet located 1,041 miles (1,666 kilometers) off the coast of east Australia. These convicts were confined to Norfolk Island because they were serving terms for more serious crimes and were more likely to be dangerous, hardened criminals. The penal colonies on the island were closed in 1855.

Another penal colony for vicious criminals was opened on the island of Tasmania, 140 miles (224 kilometers) off Australia's southeast coast. These criminals were convicts who had been transported to New South Wales to serve their terms and had then committed additional crimes. One of these convicts escaped from the settlement in 1830 and murdered six men. By the time he was recaptured, he had roasted and eaten one of his victims.

As the settlements grew, so did their problems. Farmers, many of them emancipists, found it impossible to receive a fair price for

This tower in Port Arthur, Tasmania, was part of New South Wales's own penal colony, established for convicts who broke the law while serving their original sentences in Australia. It remained in use until the end of the 19th century.

their crops from the government store, which was the only place they were permitted to sell them. The governors of the colony did not adjust the prices they paid for crops to help the farmers through seasons of drought or plenty or to store excess crops for seasons when the yield was low. Their policies made it next to impossible to make much money farming. Therefore, some farmers were forced to sell their land to officers, who consequently grew more powerful and corrupt.

The early farmers had low income and high costs, for the few trading ships that arrived at the colony charged extremely high prices for their merchandise. The settlers had no other source for provisions and were forced to pay whatever the merchants charged. When the government officers took over the supply trade to break this monopoly, the situation grew even worse. Corrupt officials re-

Farmers in the early 1800s faced an alien climate, poor soil, and thick forests of unfamiliar, useless eucalyptus trees—but they gradually succeeded in clearing and settling the land.

placed one monopoly with another and also charged high prices. They used the profit to buy land and grew still richer.

Even more demoralizing was the increasing feeling of chaos in the settlement. More and more wages were paid partly in rum. Consequently, drunkenness was rampant and violence all too common. By 1800 the community was owned by a handful of men. Most of the others either were in debt to them or worked for them. Things continued in this way for more than a decade.

In 1813 explorers found a way through the Blue Mountains, west of Sydney. Settlers flocked to the fertile land just beyond the range. In addition, in the 1820s, Australians discovered their land was nearly perfect for sheep ranching. At the same time, the British textile industry began to use many new machines and created a larger demand for wool. Raising sheep soon became a substantial source of income. Enterprising Australians started stocking their ranches with merino sheep—a Spanish breed known for its high-quality wool. The combination of economic security and the lure of unsettled land brought many settlers into Australia. Within 25 years, several settlements were established; they eventually became today's capital cities. Tasmania organized itself as a colony separate from New South Wales in 1825, and South Australia was created by a group of free settlers in 1836. From 1825 to 1845, a large number of new colonists were convicts—in fact, some people in England had begun to commit crimes just to be shipped to Australia. Still, they were outnumbered by squatters—free men and women looking for a new start who settled any uninhabited land they found, not always with legal ownership. But the middle of the 19th century brought another, even greater influx of settlers that forever changed the face and fortunes of Australia.

Gold!

In 1851 gold was discovered in both Victoria and New South Wales. Australians abandoned their farms and businesses and rushed off to seek their fortunes. Settlers from all parts of the world poured in, lured by the promise of quick riches. Many of the gold miners were men and women who had tried their luck in California during the gold rush of 1849 but had come up empty-handed. Others, however, were city dwellers who had decided to come to Australia to make an easy fortune.

In 1797, the first merino sheep were brought from South Africa to Australia, where they thrived. During the next decades, their fine wool became a staple export of the colonies. This view depicts Wentworth in New South Wales, one of the hubs of the wool trade.

Conditions in the goldfields, however, were far from easy. Most city dwellers, unused to the rigors of outdoor life, lacked the stamina to spend hours each day crouched low in a stream bed, panning for gold. Many of the would-be millionaires also lacked adequate and useful supplies—although a few had tents and pans, others attempted to pan for gold with their hats or other makeshift containers. Few could afford the licensing fees charged by the government. Those who could pay did so when officials came to collect; others, however, crept off and hid in the bush until the officials were gone.

Although conditions in the goldfields were bleak, those who were panning could hardly afford to set up camp anywhere else. Most simply set up their tents or lean-tos (wooden shacks) in little groups, returning to them at the end of each grueling day. Soon, shantytowns sprang up around goldfields. Wild and lawless, these towns were full of thieves and vagabonds willing to relieve miners of their fortunes. Professional thieves soon became known as bush-

The discovery of gold in 1851 inspired droves of Australians to leave the cities and seek their fortune in the interior. Some officials worried that Australia's newly founded industries would suffer from a lack of workers as a result.

rangers. Eventually, buildings were put up, but they were often ramshackle wooden structures little better than tents. Many miners' wives spent their days trying to keep the little shacks clean and livable while their husbands were out looking for the big strike.

Wives, however, were not the only women found around such towns. Groups of prostitutes followed the camps or settled in the shantytowns, looking for their share of the newfound wealth. Unsurprisingly, the crime rate in these towns was extremely high. Violence was a way of life. A man could lose his life over a nugget of gold, and friends turned on one another if any made a find. It was not at all unusual for a miner to strike gold only to disappear on his way to the bank to cash it in.

Harsh as conditions were for individual miners, the gold rush benefited Australia as a whole. The population of the continent increased, as settlers arrived from all over the globe, although the colonies remained predominantly British. More people meant more demand for food and equipment, and farm acreage doubled between 1850 and 1858. The gold rush also hastened the creation of a road and railroad system, although each colony built its railroads without considering connections to other colonies. As a result, the railroad tracks in different colonies were built in different widths (gauges); this hampered transportation for decades to come.

Exploration

By this time, the size and geography of Australia were better known. Throughout the 19th century, explorers opened up new areas. In 1798, Matthew Flinders and George Bass had confirmed that Tasmania (then called Van Diemen's Land) was an island separate from Australia, and Flinders sailed around the entire continent in 1803. The interior was a puzzle, however. Some explorers thought a large inland sea might cover part of it, because two rivers, the Macquarie and the Lachlan, flowed west away from the coast. In 1817, John

Australia's vast interior remained a mystery until these and other 19th-century explorers ventured into the harsh outback. One of the more fanciful theories was that an inland sea covered the center of the continent.

Oxley traveled up several rivers in New South Wales, and Charles Sturt investigated the river system of the Murrumbidgee, Darling, and Murray rivers from 1828 to 1830.

Unfortunately, none of these rivers led to useful harbors or to an inland sea. Sturt was so disappointed that the Murray River led to an outlet full of sand bars on the south coast that he wrote, "The noble river seemed to have been misplaced."

The expeditions of the 19th century confirmed that the interior was mostly dry and barren desert, but fertile plains and usable pastures were also discovered. In 1835, John Pascoe Fawkner and John Batman founded the city of Melbourne on the southeast coast, and seven years later this area was opened up to settlers. Allan Cunningham traveled north from New South Wales and discovered the area called the Darling Downs, one of the best areas for farming in Australia. During the next 50 years, expeditions crisscrossed Australia. Some returned with valuable information, some ended in tragedy. Robert Burke and William Wills successfully crossed from Melbourne in the south to the Gulf of Carpentaria on the north coast, but all but one member of their expedition died halfway through their return journey. Almost all adventurers who returned brought the same news: The land in the center of the continent was arid and bleak.

The Road to Confederation

Political awareness, as well as geographic knowledge, was growing in the colonies. Following the gold rush, the population shifted and was no longer completely centered in Sydney. Political power shifted as well. Victoria separated from New South Wales in 1851, and Queensland was divided from New South Wales in 1859. By 1856, Tasmania, South Australia, New South Wales, and Victoria had composed constitutions for themselves, subject to approval by Great Britain. Each colony allowed all men to vote for representatives to colonial legislatures, but wealthy men were allowed to vote more than once. Still, Australians strongly supported democracy.

Many laws were passed to enable small farmers to acquire land. The development of new agricultural machines, the breeding of better varieties of wheat, and the expansion of railroads allowed these farmers to prosper. In cities, in mines, and on sheep ranches, workers joined together in loose associations to demand better pay and working conditions. By 1890, labor unions were strong enough to strike and exert political pressure. Both groups, workers and farmers,

Australians voted to become a nation at the end of the 19th century. The secret-ballot system they used, in which votes are cast privately, was so unusual at that time that it became known as the Australian ballot.

contributed to the egalitarianism (belief in social, political, and economic equality) that is part of the Australian character.

In 1872 the first international telegraph line (from Darwin to Banjoewanji, Indonesia) was completed, and for the first time the continent of Australia had direct contact with the rest of the world. The country remained a group of separate colonies, however, each looking out for its own interests, with little regard for the continent as a whole. Each colony's legislature enacted different laws and tariffs (fees on exports and imports) designed to favor the products of that colony over the competing products of other colonies. The differing railroad gauges made long-distance transportation of produce and minerals difficult, and no one colony could afford to establish and support any defensive military forces.

Initial attempts at uniting the colonies were thwarted by jealousy and competition among them. Each had different needs and wants. Some wanted high protective tariffs; small colonies feared that larger colonies would dominate the federation; and colonies dependent on mining distrusted colonies populated by farmers. But after years of negotiations in the 1880s, in 1891 a convention of colonial representatives mapped out plans for a federal government that would confederate the colonies, or combine them into one nation. However, that year Australian banks began to have severe financial troubles, and soon the entire continent suffered from an unstable economy and bitter political disputes. By 1895, some people felt that confederation might help solve the economic crisis, and conventions met in 1897 and 1898 to complete the constitution. Nine years after the first convention, a continent-wide vote was held, and the colonists agreed to join together as a nation.

The Commonwealth of Australia was created in 1901, but the nation's capital, Canberra, was not founded until 1913 because of rivalry between the former colonies. This aerial view of the modern capital shows the National Library in the foreground; Parliament House is behind it.

Australia in the 20th Century

On January 1, 1901, the British Parliament approved the constitution drawn up by the Australian colonies and created the Commonwealth of Australia. This new nation included the former colonies of New South Wales, Queensland, Tasmania, Victoria, South Australia, and Western Australia. (The area north of South Australia, between Western Australia and Queensland, became the Northern Territory in 1911.) But ties with the parent country, Great Britain, remained strong. Indeed, most of the states trusted Great Britain more than they trusted each other. Each state was accustomed to British rule, and each suspected all the others of looking out for their own interests at the expense of the whole. A new national capital, Canberra, had to be built and the capital territory put under federal control because no state wanted another state to house the capital.

On the subject of immigration, however, all the states thought alike. In Queensland, in the northern part of the continent, the tropical climate is best suited to raising sugarcane. Many Polynesians (called Kanakas, from the Hawaiian word for "person") were employed by the farmers there by the end of the 19th century, but Australians resented their presence, fearing they would work for cheaper wages than Australians and take jobs away from citizens. In

1906 and 1907, the government sent most of the Kanakas home. This was the first effort to preserve "White Australia," and for decades afterward an extremely discriminatory immigration policy prevented Asians from moving to Australia while it encouraged Caucasians, especially people from Great Britain, to do so.

Part of the pressure to expel the Kanakas came from the highly organized labor movement that gained political power in the first decades of the 20th century. Unions of sheep shearers, dockworkers, and miners were established in the 1890s; by the 1910s, many labor leaders had been elected as members of state legislatures, where they pushed for the passage of laws protecting high wages, limiting the number of work hours per week, and regulating working conditions. Australia's labor laws were some of the world's most advanced, and the country could claim to be ahead of most other nations in another way as well: In 1902 it became the second nation in the world in which women gained the right to vote.

By the time Australia became independent, labor unions were both strong and well organized. Associations of industrial workers, sheepshearers, and dockworkers, among others, helped elect legislators who passed laws regulating working conditions.

The new nation soon began to develop its economy. In 1905 the first blast furnace for producing steel was opened, and in 1915 the Broken Hills Proprietary Company opened the first of the steel plants that made it one of Australia's most successful corporations. Australia was at last able to make use of its vast deposits of iron ore, and industrial development leaped forward. That year also marked another milestone in Australia's growth as a nation, for Australian military forces engaged in combat for the first time.

The legislature had created an Australian navy in 1909, and a policy of mandatory military training had begun. The new troops were put to the test when Australia entered World War I. Britain, France, and Russia, later joined by the United States and others, fought together as the Allies against the Central Powers, which included Germany, Austria-Hungary, Bulgaria, and the Ottoman Empire (part of which is now Turkey). As a part of the British Commonwealth, Australia entered the war in 1914. On April 25, 1915, at Gallipoli (a peninsula in the Dardanelles near the border of present-day Turkey and Greece) the Australia and New Zealand Army Corps (ANZAC) troops landed and joined in a battle against the Turks. During the 8 months of fighting at Gallipoli, which ended in an Allied defeat, Australia lost more than 8,000 men but gained an international reputation as a nation of brave soldiers. A total of 329,000 Australians went overseas in World War I, and 60,000 died in combat or from combat-related injuries. The total of 226,000 casualties was the highest casualty rate of all the British forces. Australia actually lost more soldiers than the United States in the war—but gained a sense of national identity.

The 1920s were marked by economic progress. Travel around the enormous continent grew easier as cars became more common and roads were built and improved. Electric trains ferried workers to and from jobs in the rapidly expanding cities. The iron and steel industries boomed, but agriculture did not. Droughts caused crops

Fighting in the Pacific in World War II directly threatened Australia. The nation turned to the United States for help in beating back the Japanese invasion of Pacific islands.

to fail for several years, and by the time the droughts had ended in the 1930s, the world was in the grip of a severe depression. Other nations could afford less of the raw materials and agricultural products that Australia exported, and prices fell. Money was scarce, businesses failed, and in some areas as many as 30 percent of workers could not find jobs.

In 1939, Australia entered World War II. Once again, Australian soldiers showed their bravery on the battlefields. They fought as part of the British Commonwealth on the side of the Allies, which included France, the United States, and the Soviet Union, against the Axis powers of Nazi Germany, Italy, and Japan. World War II marked a turning point in Australia's history, for Japanese forces were active in the Pacific and for the first time the Australian continent itself was directly threatened by military attack. Japanese submarines reached Sydney harbor, and the Japanese bombed the northern city of Darwin in 1942. This time the fighting was close to home.

Until this point, the Australians had paid little attention to their Asian neighbors, but World War II changed that. When the Japanese bombed Pearl Harbor in Hawaii, Australia was forced to acknowledge that Japan was a very real threat. Australia fully supported Great Britain throughout the war, but it was the United States that stationed troops in Australia to protect the country, and it was the American navy that defended Australia. Australian forces battled beside U.S. air and sea forces in the brutal, hard-fought battles against Japanese occupation of the Pacific islands. The death toll was high: More than 30,000 Australian soldiers died in the fighting.

After World War II, the country set about building a solid peacetime economy. The war had cut Australia off from its trading partners, so its own industries were forced to manufacture the goods Australia needed, spurring economic growth. Social welfare services such as unemployment benefits, disability payments (for those disabled or too ill to work), and national health coverage were created. Air transportation was finally recognized as a necessity, and the National Airlines Act of 1945 established Trans-Australia Airlines, a government-owned airline. Job placement programs were started for servicemen and -women returning home from the war, and free university education was offered.

After the appalling Holocaust (mass killing of the Jews at the hands of the Nazis in World War II), people around the world began to reconsider racism and racist policies. In Australia this meant a gradual easing in the 1950s of the White Australia policy.

Citizens of Australia also realized that more immigrants were needed to populate the country. To encourage immigration, the Australian government offered free passage to former servicemen and -women from other countries as well as reduced fares to others who wanted to settle in Australia. From the end of World War II in 1945 to 1970, close to 3 million people arrived in Australia. Although almost half of the immigrants were British, the rest were from countries that had sustained great damage in the war. Many were Italians, Yugoslavs, and Greeks.

The next decade saw still more discoveries of mineral resources. Oil and natural gas were found in Queensland, the Bass Strait, and Western Australia. New markets for Australia's products were explored as well. Japan's phenomenal industrial growth made it a customer for Australian iron and steel; China began importing Australian wheat to feed its enormous population; and the textile mills of Japan, South Korea, and Taiwan became steady buyers of Australian wool.

The aborigines, for so long excluded from Australian politics, society, and wealth, at last began to have some power on the national scene. Although aborigines had lived in Australia for thousands of years, they were not allowed to vote, and the government did not even count them in the national census. Inspired in part by Native Americans' struggle for rights in the United States, they began to demand recognition. In 1962, they gained the right to vote and five years later were included in the national census. Yet despite a string of federal court decisions restoring some of their original land and recognizing sacred sites, they have far to go toward gaining equality.

Vietnam Involvement

Asian nations engaged Australia's attention in the 1960s in many ways. When France withdrew its troops from its former colony of Vietnam in Southeast Asia, groups of Vietnamese fought for control of the region, and the struggle soon became violent. A Communist government controlled northern Vietnam; a non-Communist government controlled the south. The United States supported the south.

As a member of SEATO (the Southeast Asia Treaty Organization, which also included the United States, France, New Zealand, Pakistan, the Philippines, Thailand, and Great Britain), Australia had

During the 1960s, aborigines protested for civil rights. These marchers belong to the Gurindji tribe.

pledged to come to the aid of certain territories if they were threatened by a Communist takeover. One such territory was southern Vietnam. In May 1962, under the provisions of the SEATO pact, 30 Australian army instructors were sent to train South Vietnamese troops. This marked the beginning of Australian involvement in the Vietnam War.

In 1964, Australia doubled the number of its advisers to 60. In 1965, troops were sent to Vietnam. Some observers believe that Australia decided to enter the Vietnam confrontation only because the United States was involved. Many Australians believed that they should help the United States so that the United States would, in return, help defend Australia against any future Asian invasion.

In 1966 the United States asked Australia for more support in the Vietnam conflict and was promptly rewarded with an additional 4,500 troops. By 1972, however, to the relief of many citizens who had protested their country's involvement, Australia had completely withdrawn from the fighting in Vietnam.

Facing the Next Century

Australia reduced its commitment to immigration in 1974, when restrictions were imposed. Problems in the world economy were reflected in Australia, and joblessness was high. The country could no longer welcome anyone who wished to come and make a living in Australia, for the Australians themselves were having a hard time doing so. The new policies established preferred classes of immigrants: Applicants are ranked by age, educational level, number of dependents, and useful skills. Young men and women without children who are adequately educated and can perform jobs necessary to the economy are preferred.

These soldiers belonged to the Second Royal Australian Regiment, which was part of the Australian forces in Vietnam. Some Australians objected to their nation's role in the conflict, just as Americans argued over the United States's involvement in Vietnam.

Mineral discoveries in the 1960s boosted the Australian economy to new heights. The Kambalda nickel mine, shown here, is in Western Australia.

At the same time that the government reduced immigration, it began to return land to the continent's original residents. In 1992, a court decision for the first time recognized the rights of aborigines as first owners of the land. By the late 1990s, roughly half of the Northern Territory, 20 percent of South Australia, 10 percent of Western Australia, and smaller sections of Queensland and New South Wales had been returned to aboriginal control. Yet the complicated settlements, involving combinations of outright ownership, leasing of the land, mining rights, and forms of tribal government, severely diluted the aborigines' gains.

In addition to the usual water hazards and sand traps, Australian golfers may have to cope with kangaroos browsing on the course.

The Aussies

As a group, the Aussies (as the Australians are nicknamed) are no longer as homogenous as they once were. The end of the White Australia policy in the 1950s, together with various types of bonuses to immigrants after World War II, opened up Australia to a flood of new citizens in the middle of the 20th century. Today, Australia is an ethnic melting pot—a country rich with diverse cultures. In fact, nearly 5 million of Australia's more than 18 million citizens are immigrants.

For the most part, the rest of the Australians can trace their roots back to Great Britain, most from England, some from Ireland—maybe even as far back as one of the original convict settlers. And although in the past two centuries Australia sometimes seemed as British as Britain, today Australia has a style and culture all its own.

When settlers built towns and cities in the late 18th and early 19th centuries, most built homes that resembled the ones they had left behind. Consequently, whole towns can still be found filled with fine examples of Victorian and Gothic architecture. Unfortunately, these high-ceilinged, tall, thin homes were more suited to England's damp climate than to Australia's balmy temperatures. Therefore

This livestock worker on the Fossil Downs Station in Western Australia has more comfortable quarters than the rough shacks that housed the pioneers of the outback.

many of the houses were oppressively hot, looked out of place in the landscape, and made little use of Australia's abundant sunshine. Later architects designed homes better suited to the hot, dry weather. The most popular models are low, sprawling ranch-type structures with tile roofs.

The majority of Australian citizens—60 percent—live in homes they own. Home ownership is perhaps the one goal common to almost all Australians. It is not unusual for even very young couples to own their residence. These houses are likely to be in the suburbs that encircle the major cities and are often surrounded by well-kept lawns and gardens that reflect the Australians' passion for outdoor life and leisure.

For the most part, although fortunes have been made there, Australia does not have many large, ostentatious estates. Almost all Australians, including the well-to-do, consider themselves middle class and live accordingly—a reflection of their egalitarian attitude.

Contrary to the popular media image of the typical Australian—bronzed, tough, living in the outback, and wrestling crocodiles—85 percent of Australians live in or around cities. In fact, nearly half of the nation's population lives in or around the two cities of Sydney and Melbourne. Only 180,000 people live in the barren Northern Territory, and most of them live either in its capital, Darwin, or in "the Alice," the city of Alice Springs. The capital of Queensland, Brisbane, is home to about 1.5 million residents; South Australia's capital, Adelaide, houses 1.1 million; Western Australia has 1.5 million residents, 1.2 million of whom live in its capital, Perth; and Hobart, the capital of Tasmania, is Australia's second oldest city and has 200,000 residents. The remainder of the population — only 15 percent — is scattered throughout the outback or lives in smaller, rural settlements.

Holidays and Festivals

Australians enjoy their leisure time. In fact, they have more of it than the people of many industrialized nations (including the United States). Most Australians receive several weeks off each year with a substantial vacation bonus in pay, which allows them to explore their country. National holidays include Christmas, New Year's Day (also Australian Independence Day), ANZAC Day (commemorating the Allied landing at Gallipoli), and Easter.

In addition to these nationally celebrated holidays, there are a number of local festivals and holidays throughout the nation. In New South Wales, January is the Festival of Sydney, marked by a month of special events ranging from jazz concerts to fireworks displays. In Victoria, the Dragon Boat Festival is held at Easter in the capital city of Melbourne. This festival features paddleboat races on the Yarra River and is designed to help residents better understand Chinese culture. In October, in the town of Bowen in Queensland, the Gem of the Coral Coast Festival takes place. This festival begins with a blessing of fishing boats and ends with a tomato-eating contest. In South Australia in the town of Hahndorf, the second Saturday in January is always the Schuetzenfest. This is a typical German feast— complete with German foods, beer, and dancing. In Western Australia, Shinju Matsuri (the Festival of the Pearl) is celebrated each January in the town of Broome, which was settled by pearl fishers. A celebration of the town's past, the festival includes colorful Chinese dragons and the Sayonara Ball. Perhaps the strangest festival of all takes place in Darwin, the capital of the Northern Territory. Each June its residents gather for the annual Beer Can Regatta. As the name suggests, the contestants race boats made of beer cans.

Sports and Recreation

But as much as Australians enjoy their festivals and, in general, take things pretty lightly, in one area they are deadly serious: sports. Given the fact that 75 percent of Australians live within 50 miles (80 kilometers) of the shore, the large number of beaches, and the warm weather of most regions, it is no wonder that water sports are wildly popular. Rival beach clubs hold "iron man" races in which participants compete on a course that involves swimming and paddling both a surfboard and a surf-ski. Serious surfers can make an exhilarating living touring the international surfing circuit and honing their skill in the world-renowned ocean rollers at home.

The 1986 America's Cup races were held in Australian waters. Here, the boat Australia III *(bottom) rounds a marker ahead of its competition.*

Another Australian passion is for boats—of any size or shape. A 1982 survey counted more than 150,000 yachtsmen and 100,000 speedboat owners in Australia. The America's Cup, a prestigious cup awarded to the winner of a series of yachting races, was held by the United States for 132 years, until the Australian yacht *Australia II* gained the prize in 1983. Australia's success in that race is still a matter of national pride, and the America's Cup race is one of the most popular sporting events viewed in Australia.

An 1886 engraving shows an audience of elegantly dressed colonists watching bicycle riders at the Melbourne Cricket Ground. Even today, Melbourne retains an old-fashioned, Victorian air.

Cricket, a British game somewhat resembling baseball, is one of the national sports of Australia—one most fans take very seriously. Played during the summer months, a test (international) match lasts for five days, although a shorter, one-day version has recently been introduced. During the winter months local leagues play many versions of football, soccer, and rugby. Australia's own contribution to spectator sports is Australian Rules Football, played by 18-member teams on an oversize field.

Australia has produced more than its share of excellent tennis players as well. The Australian team claimed the Davis Cup, awarded to the victors in the most prestigious team-tennis event in the world, 20 times between 1939 and 1986. Nearly 40 Wimbledon winners came from Australia, and the history of the sport could not be told without including the names of Margaret Court, Ken Rosewall, Rod Laver, John David Newcombe, and Evonne Goolagong Cawley—all Australians.

Dining

For the most part, Australians enjoy a leisurely life with emphasis on the outdoors. This may mean hiking and camping in one of the numerous national parks or simply enjoying a barbecue with neighbors in the backyard. The barbecue, or "barbie," has become almost as much a part of the Australian image as koalas or kangaroos. Barbecues are located in public parks, portable models are carried by hikers, and various built-in and store-bought models range from the reasonably to the outrageously priced. Barbecue cuisine can range from casual burgers or sausages to gourmet shrimp in wine or chicken with herbs. But whatever the meal, barbecues have become the perfect accompaniment to a way of life based on leisure and the great outdoors.

Aside from barbecued foods, a variety of cuisines can be found in Australia. The large groups of immigrants that came to the country brought their own cultures with them. And what better way to share cultures than by sharing food? Throughout the country and particularly in the major cities, especially Melbourne, restaurants serving Italian, French, American, Japanese, Greek, Chinese, and vegetarian fare are easy to find.

There is, however, little in the way of specifically Australian cuisine. Most of the first settlers could barely scratch an existence from the land, much less devise innovative recipes. Food was often overcooked, lumpy, tasteless, and drowned in gravy. Today, although there are a few regional specialties, the only thing that comes close to a national food is the meat pie. However, Australian wines are a national pride and have begun to win international recognition.

The aborigines did create a few uniquely Australian dishes. They may not appeal to the weak of stomach, but these foods are available in some restaurants in Australia. They include witchetty grubs, honey ants, and kangaroo. Witchetty grubs are actually the white larvae of wood-boring beetles, each about as long as an index finger. Aborigine women use long sticks to expose the roots of bushes and plants, where these grubs may be found. Then they break the roots apart to expose the pinkish white flesh of the grubs. The grubs are eaten alive and are said to have a creamy, buttery taste. Honey ants are dug from their storage chambers beneath the earth. Aborigines enjoy the round little ants, which are bloated with sweet honey, by the handful. Kangaroos are hunted both for their meat and for their fur. Traditionally, an aborigine hunter hurled a boomerang (curved wooden weapon) and used a woomera (throwing stick) to launch spears with deadly accuracy. The aborigines had few weapons, but their store included several varieties of boomerangs. The kind of boomerang that returns to the thrower is mostly used in games.

Aborigine Life

Aborigine culture differs greatly from that of the rest of Australia. In recent years, it has moved to the forefront of Australia's art and literature. Aborigine art is currently displayed in galleries and museums and is sold at stands throughout the country. Ancient cave and rock paintings—some of them 5,000 years old—have been uncovered and are protected by law. Aborigine myths and tales of Dreamtime are becoming an acknowledged part of Australian heritage. Although aborigines had no written literature, their rich oral tradition preserved their stories in the form of long songs, often recited at corroborees, celebrations where up to 1,000 aborigines gathered for dancing, singing, and socializing.

Of the somewhat more than 200,000 aborigines now living in Australia, the majority live on reserves or native land, while perhaps

This aborigine family in central Australia lives on a reserve of tribal land. Other aborigines dwell in the coastal cities, often in slums. Today, aborigines are demanding a greater share in Australia's prosperity and a greater role in government.

100,000 live in cities and urban slums. Although they have been granted a large portion of land in the Northern Territory, most aborigines feel that the Australian government has far to go before it makes up for hundreds of years of brutality and oppression. For example, until 1939 in the state of New South Wales, anyone who had aborigine blood could be forced to live on a reserve. Such people could not own land, they needed government permission to take jobs, and they were required to hand over their earnings to a government supervisor. The aborigines of Tasmania fared worse—they were completely eradicated by 1876. The tale of the aborigines' suffering at the hands of the European colonists is filled with stories of death, mistreatment, and sickness, for they had no immunity to diseases the settlers brought. Today the urban slums are still marked by inadequate health care. Although a number of aborigines now hold key governmental positions, true equality has not yet been achieved.

Religion

At one time the majority of Australians were members of the Church of England, or Anglicans. Today Catholics make up an equal part of the population of churchgoers. Close to 26 percent of Australians are Catholic. Roughly the same number (26 percent) are Anglicans. There are growing communities of both Jewish and Greek Orthodox worshipers. In addition, an increasing number of Australians profess no religion at all — more than 1 million of them.

A Different Way of Life

Although urban Australians lead lives resembling those of city dwellers in other industrialized countries—featuring houses in the suburbs, cars, televisions, and telephones—a few live in a uniquely Australian manner. Life on a sheep or cattle ranch in the outback is very different from life in a city.

Many people think the outback is a vast, barren wasteland and—for the most part—it deserves this reputation. But pockets of civilization exist there. Some are encampments of aborigine tribes; some are the cattle and sheep ranches for which Australia is famous. Because the land is so bleak, each animal requires many acres of pasture, and the ranches are consequently quite large. On these huge ranches, life can be difficult. Wild animals prey on the herds and

Ranches such as this cattle station in Queensland often cover enormous areas, because the sparse vegetation means that each cow or sheep needs to graze over plenty of land. Some stations are several days' travel by car from one end to the other.

flocks, ranchers and animals can be lost in the wilderness, and the lack of rain is a constant threat. In a prolonged drought, entire herds may have to be destroyed or sold for a fraction of their value.

Although conditions on these ranches are somewhat primitive and the isolation is quite severe, ranch life in the outback appeals to some people. Contrary to the popular media image, however, there is very little glamour in getting up before dawn, feeding and herding animals all day long, and spending days surrounded by wool during shearing time. There are also few creature comforts in the outback, and ranch hands are likely to sleep in bunk houses, much as American cowboys once did. In order to herd the animals, most hands ride horses or all-terrain vehicles. Although the ranches are few and far between, towns do spring up around groups of ranches. Often, the towns are not much more than a general store where ranchers can pick up supplies, mail letters, and do a bit of socializing.

There is also little that is glamorous about the lives of the residents of Coober Pedy—although the entire town is devoted to mining gems. Located in the territory of South Australia, Coober Pedy is the world's largest opal-producing town. The temperatures there can reach 122° F (50° C). To avoid the scorching heat and seek some relief from the glare of the sun, residents go underground.

In the outback, horses can often go where cars and trucks cannot. Ranchers herd their stock on horseback, and tourists can arrange mounted excursions into the bush.

Houses, hotels, businesses, and churches are all located under the earth, where a thriving suburban community exists. Even weddings and festivals take place underground. Most of the town's socializing goes on underground as well, and most homes are outfitted with all the modern conveniences. In fact, if the town were uncovered, it would look much like any other Australian suburb.

John Howard became Australia's prime minister in 1996 as a result of the Liberal/National Country coalition's defeat of the Labor Party, which had held power since 1983.

Government

Late in the 19th century, the six British colonies in Australia were governed separately. Each had certain rights of self-government under a constitution, and each had a group of elected representatives who had power to pass laws regarding affairs within the colony. All foreign relations were controlled by Great Britain, and the British Parliament retained a miscellaneous assortment of powers to approve or veto colonial legislation. This peculiarly British system was called responsible government.

During the late 1800s, Australians realized the benefits they would gain if they became one unified nation. The constitution that was eventually drawn up and approved by the British Parliament in 1901 is the one under which Australia is governed today as a democratic federation of states. The constitution reflects the country's British ancestry, but it also strongly reflects democratic ideals. It includes elements of both the British parliamentary system and the U.S. federal system.

Elements of the British system are apparent in the duties of the British monarch as head of state, the duties of the monarch's representatives, and the office of prime minister.

The Australian flag (featuring a small Union Jack in one corner as a tribute to Great Britain) waves over the courtyard of the federal Parliament House in Canberra; the nation's coat of arms is mounted above the central doorway.

The influence of the U.S. federal system is evident in the separation of executive, legislative, and judicial powers and in the roles of the federal and state governments.

The king or queen of England is the official head of state and has formal executive powers but no direct authority over Australian laws and government. The monarch is represented in Australia by the governor-general, who is appointed on the recommendation of elected Australian officials. The governor-general rarely exercises authority, though in 1975 Sir John Kerr dismissed the Labor government, a controversial action (formally, he did appoint the prime minister). As in Great Britain and Canada, the prime minister is the leader of the party that has the most members in the legislature, or Parliament. The cabinet is a group of advisers selected by the prime minister from members of Parliament. In theory, state governors are also representatives of the British monarch although they, too, are appointed on the recommendation of Australian officials.

Legislative (lawmaking) power is held by Parliament, which is divided into an upper house and lower house. The upper house, called the Senate, has 76 members: 12 from each state and 2 from each territory. Senators from states serve six-year terms; senators from territories serve three-year terms. Every three years an election is held for half of the Senate's seats, so that the entire Senate is not replaced every six years. The lower house, or House of Representatives, has 148 members, each elected for a 3-year term. The upper and lower houses have equal legislative powers except for one important area—only the House of Representatives can propose and pass bills that affect government money and spending.

Australia is composed of six states (New South Wales, Victoria, Queensland, South Australia, Western Australia, and Tasmania) and two territories (the Northern Territory and the Australian Capital Territory). Powers not held by the federal government are delegated to the states, each of which has a governor, who represents the king or queen, and its own legislature and judicial system. The Northern Territory and Queensland have one-chamber legislatures. All the other states have two-chamber legislatures in which the upper house is called the legislative council and the lower house is called either the legislative assembly or the house of assembly. The head of a state government is called a premier. Any citizen over 18 years of age can vote; voting is mandatory for parliamentary elections.

The seat of the federal government is in Canberra, an area that was given by New South Wales to the federal government to become the Australian Capital Territory in 1911. The duties of the federal government are quite separate from those of the state governments and include defense, national economic policy, and foreign relations. The state governments are responsible for police, education, and social welfare. Local governments have very little power. Most of them are responsible only for regulating building codes and for town planning and zoning.

The judicial system consists of local or circuit courts, magistrates' courts, county courts, children's courts, and higher state courts. Cases are first tried in one of these court systems. Capital crimes (murder, felonies, and other serious crimes) are tried before a state supreme court. The High Court of Australia is the highest court in the land as well as the official interpreter of the constitution. The High Court consists of a chief justice and six fellow justices.

There are several political parties in Australia, each embracing a political philosophy slightly different from the others. Basically, these parties are either for or against labor organizations. Labor unions have a long history of power in Australia, and their influence has done much to help workers and to encourage the passage of social welfare laws. The influence of labor unions is opposed by parties that are supported by farmers and industrialists. Australia's three largest political parties are the Labor party, the Liberal party, and the National Country party. In the late 1990s, a Liberal/National Country coalition ousted Labor, which had held power for 13 years.

Although there is no draft in Australia (meaning that army service is not required), the Australian Regular Army has more than 25,000 enlistees. The Royal Australian Navy has 15,000 servicemen and -women; the Royal Australian Air Force has more than 18,000 in uniform. Reserve forces are also available in case of a national emergency.

Australia belongs to one major military alliance: the ANZUS (Australia, New Zealand, and the United States) military pact. Prob-

(continued on p. 89)

SCENES OF
AUSTRALIA

◄ *Brightly lit skyscrapers illuminate Perth's skyline at night. Mineral wealth in Western Australia has fueled the city's growth in recent years.*

Λ *Sailboards fill the harbor with a rainbow of colors during a race at the annual Festival of Sydney. Australians love outdoor sports and holidays; this popular festival combines both and is one of many the Aussies and foreign tourists alike enthusiastically attend.*

➤ *The caves and rocks of the Northern Territory are the site of many celebrated aborigine art works, including the Blue Paintings, parts of which are shown at right.*

⋏ *Australia's long stretches of coast, coral reefs, and offshore islands attract sun worshipers from all over. The shore features some spectacular beaches, bays, and coves including those of Lizard Island, shown here.*

⋏ *On the southern coast, this island archway formed by the pounding surf rises from the ocean near Victoria.*

ʌ *Enormous, smooth, rounded boulders lie strewn in piles in parts of Australia's barren interior. This group is known as the Devil's Marbles.*

◄ *Huge colonies of termites built these strange-looking mounds in the bush in the Northern Territory. Some mounds are six feet (two meters) tall.*

⋀ and ⋁ Although most Australians live in cities, some prefer life on the grassy plains that support Australia's large number of livestock. Above: a herdsman drives horses in the outback. Below: sheep ranchers inspect members of their flock.

⋏ *The outdoor-loving Aussies are avid sports fans and players. These young enthusiasts attending the Victoria Football League Grand Final proudly display scarves bearing the team colors, face paint, and buttons picturing their favorite players.*

⋏ *Although Australia is the driest inhabited continent, verdant hills and valleys can be found, such as those surrounding this red-roofed farm near Kiama, a few miles south of Sydney on the southwestern coast.*

(continued from p. 80)

lems in this alliance developed in 1984, when New Zealand declared that vessels bearing nuclear arms or powered by nuclear energy were not allowed in its ports. The United States strongly objected, because many of its naval vessels would be barred from docking in New Zealand. As a result, Australia and the United States suspended New Zealand's participation in ANZUS and held bilateral meetings instead.

Australia is a member of the British Commonwealth of Nations and the United Nations; it participates in the Colombo Plan, a program for aiding development in India, Pakistan, and other Asian nations.

Social Services

The single largest part of the federal budget is devoted to social security payments. Indeed, Australia was one of the world's first countries to adopt a social welfare plan. In 1909, Australia provided pensions for the elderly; a year later it added pensions for people too sick to work. In 1912, maternity allowances (money paid to pregnant women for health care) were introduced. Individual states are responsible for certain social welfare programs, including housing and public health.

Australia also offers a free public education system to its more than 3 million children. The system has 3 levels: elementary (from 6 to 12 years of age), secondary (from age 12 to age 15 or 16), and tertiary (college or university level). There are also a number of expensive private schools, including military schools. The arrival of waves of immigrants, many of whom were not Protestants, spurred the creation of a number of private, religious institutions. Today, almost 1,000,000 children attend private schools. In Australia, children are required by law to attend one of the more than 7,000 government-run or more than 2,000 private schools until they are at least 15 years of age (16 in Tasmania).

Children who live in the outback are often too far from any school to attend classes, and children with disabilities sometimes find it difficult to attend a regular school. In answer to these problems, the Australian government created Schools of the Air. These schools send lessons and homework through the mail and also use

In August of 1988, the government announced plans to change the funding and structure of the public school system in New South Wales. More than 50,000 teachers, students, and parents gathered in Sydney to protest the changes. Despite this enthusiasm, the dropout rate is high.

two-way radios to allow students and teachers to communicate during regular school hours. Australia has 38 universities, most of which are run by the government, plus a variety of colleges and technical colleges.

Although Australia has a well-educated population—almost every Australian over the age of 10 can read and write—many people worry that more attention should be paid to education in order to prepare coming generations for the future. Nearly 95 percent of all 17 year olds in Japan are students; in Australia, only 40 percent of 17 year olds are students. Figures such as these are an ominous sign that Australia must make a greater effort to keep pace and compete successfully with its neighbors.

Health Care

Perhaps the most unique feature of Australian health services is the Royal Flying Doctor Service, designed for residents of the outback. This service provides medical care to outlying areas through the use of two-way radios and a fleet of almost 40 airplanes. Doctors use the radios to keep in contact with their patients; the planes are used when medical attention is required.

All Australians are covered by a system of universal health insurance that pays 85 percent of the government-set rate for medical services provided by private doctors. Outpatient treatment is free, and hospital charges are covered when the patient is in a public hospital and is cared for by physicians employed there; private medical insurance is also available. The government owns 75 percent of the nation's more than 1,000 hospitals. There are more than 75,000 hospital beds in Australia, and more than 42,000 physicians. The average life expectancy of women is 83 years; of men, 76 years (life expectancy is the number of years someone can expect to live). The

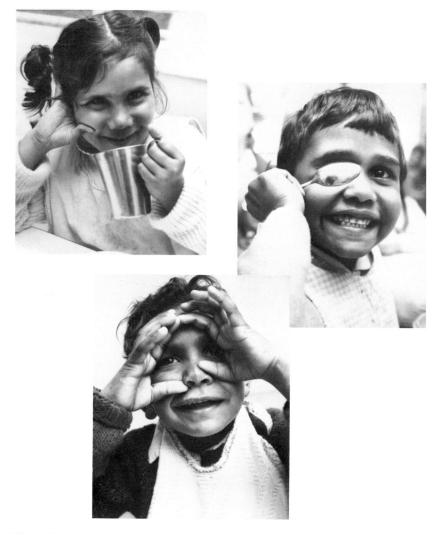

These three young aborigines have just received medical care at Far West Children's Health Scheme Home, one of the health facilities set up to serve residents of the outback. The children have had to travel a long distance from their homes to reach a hospital, so they will live at this facility until their treatment is complete.

infant mortality rate is 5.5 per 1,000 live births (infant mortality refers to the number of children who die during their first year). These figures compare well to the rates for other modern industrialized nations. For the most part, Australians are a healthy group of people. The most frequently occurring disease is the common cold. The most common cause of death in the country is atherosclerosis, a degenerative disease that starts with the building up of fatty deposits in the arteries in the body.

One public health problem is alcohol consumption. Australia has the third-highest beer consumption rate in the world: Its citizens drink an average of 38 gallons of beer a year per person. Of course, consumption varies widely from person to person, and even from region to region. Residents of Darwin in the north, for example, average 60 gallons of beer per year. In recent years, the high rate of alcohol-related automobile fatalities has caused stricter enforcement of drunk-driving laws. Australia's nearness to Southeast Asia, where opium poppies are grown, has made the opium derivative heroin the country's most frequently abused illegal drug.

Melbourne's harbor, like the harbors at Sydney and Perth, is one of the world's greatest centers of international shipping.

Economy, Transportation, and Communications

The economic history of Australia closely resembles a ride on a roller coaster. Cycles of "boom" and "bust" follow one another as the economy alternately expands and contracts. The original settlers faced unfamiliar, barren land and struggled to produce enough food simply to feed themselves and their families. In the 1820s the introduction of sheep farming provided a new way to make a living. Land that would not support farming was used as grazing land. As the continent was explored, travelers found land suited to cattle raising, and many settlers started cattle ranches. At midcentury the gold rush of 1851 provoked an enormous boom as immigrants and money flooded into Australia. Some miners made fortunes, and entire towns were built on the proceeds. It seemed that Australia was a land of unlimited opportunity. But then the flood of wealth turned into a trickle, and the trickle dried up. When gold fever wore off, settlers were once again forced to make their living by farming and ranching. Cattle ranches and sheep farms were soon the main source of income. Soon Australia was not only feeding itself but also had become a major supplier of food to other nations.

Throughout the second half of the 19th century, the various colonial governments tried to encourage the growth of industry by imposing protective tariffs. Tariffs are fees placed on imported goods, thus making such goods more expensive. Australian industry did benefit somewhat from this protectionist policy, which has continued through most of Australia's history.

The discovery of large deposits of valuable minerals fueled another boom. Exploitation of the continent's vast stores of iron ore, coal, and other mineral resources spurred industrial growth in the 1920s. The worldwide depression that followed was disastrous for the farmers and ranchers, however, as the prices paid for wheat and wool were cut in half. Despite the misery of the depression, industrial development took place because producers were forced to become more efficent in order to make any profit. By 1939, manufactured goods made up twice as much of the gross national product (total value of all goods and services produced by a country) as they had in 1911. During World War II, Australia became a true industrialized nation when it was forced to produce many kinds of finished goods it formerly imported.

After World War II, the nation experienced nearly 25 years of economic growth. Additional discoveries of minerals made Australia a leading raw material exporter, shipping and selling minerals to other countries. Freer immigration policies increased the work force. The 1960s ushered in a period of tremendous economic growth. Markets opened up for all of Australia's agricultural products. Oil was discovered in the Bass Strait, and iron ore deposits in Western Australia brought profitable contracts with steel companies in Japan. Whereas once Australia's import and export trade had been mostly with Great Britain, Asian and South Pacific countries became increasingly important trading partners. The economic future looked bright.

A mine at Weipa, in a remote part of the Cape York Peninsula, produces bauxite. This and other mineral resources—including gold, iron ore, and oil—have given the Australian economy some much-needed boosts.

During the 1970s, however, growth slowed dramatically. Inflation and unemployment rates both began to rise, and the oil crisis of the early 1970s caused a worldwide economic slowdown that reduced markets for Australia's exports. However, some of Australia's economic troubles in the 1980s and early 1990s arose from problems within the country.

Some observers believe that the strong labor unions had damaged Australia's ability to compete in the world marketplace. Strikes were frequent, and the strikers often won higher wages and shorter hours. This, in turn, drove up the price of merchandise so that the manufacturer could still make a profit. These conditions made it virtually impossible for Australia to compete effectively with the manufacturing power of the Asian nations, particularly Japan, where

Today, commerce and sales play an ever-growing part in Australia's economic life, as tourism and trade increase and manufacturing decreases. Many young Australians seek work in shops and restaurants rather than in factories or mines.

there was a large cheap labor supply and production could continue around the clock.

In most Australian industries, workers generally work only 40 hours (30 in some industries). Although productivity has increased markedly in recent years, in part because of a new spirit of cooperation shown by the labor movement, Australia still faces many difficulties in becoming competitive in the global marketplace. For example, jobs that demand more complex operations require trained workers. But, faced with additional training, many workers are leaving manufacturing to work in easier industries. Experts fear that the increase in tourism (almost 4 million people visit Australia each year) and the service businesses such as hotels, restaurants, golf clubs, and discos that are associated with tourism may be undermining the manufacturing industries. Currently, industry is declining compared with the meteoric rise of tourism and related businesses. Critics point out that Australians obsessed with living stress-free lives of leisure may be turning to easier, less-challenging jobs.

By the late 1990s, 8 percent of Australians had no jobs, and the unemployment rate among the young (ages 16–20) was more than twice as high. However, the inflation rate had dropped below 5 percent, bringing it more in line with that of other modern industrialized nations.

Improvement in technology is one answer to sparking growth. In the past, Australia has lagged behind many nations in technological expertise, but that gap is narrowing. To challenge its competitors, Australia has recognized that it must use new technology to speed up production and efficiency of the work force.

Japan is Australia's major overall trading partner, but Japan's own economic problems have somewhat reduced its influence. By the late 1990s, Japan was buying over 20 percent of all Australian exports and providing close to 15 percent of imports (down from a high of nearly 25 percent). Japanese investors, recognizing Australia's potential, have bought businesses and real estate in Australia, and many Australians resent this extension of foreign influence.

Structure of the Economy

Despite current economic problems, Australia's diversified economy allows its residents to enjoy a fairly high standard of living, with one of the highest rates of car and home ownership in the world.

The yearly income per person is $21,000, which compares well with figures from the United States and Western European nations. The basic unit of currency is the Australian dollar ($A), which is divided into 100 cents. The monetary system is very similar to that of the United States, although the Australian dollar is worth more than the U.S. dollar on the world market. ($A 1.00 was equal to about U.S. $1.35 in the late 1990s.)

Australia's major trading partners are Japan and the United States, followed by the United Kingdom, South Korea, and New Zealand. The leading purchasers of Australian exports are Japan (20 percent), the United States (11 percent), and South Korea and New Zealand (roughly 6 percent each). The United States has passed Japan at providing Australian imports (23 percent to Japan's 15 percent), followed by the United Kingdom (7 percent). The manufacturing sector — never the largest employer — has declined somewhat further. By the late 1990s, roughly 70 percent of the labor force worked in commerce and services, 14 percent in manufacturing, 7 percent in construction, and about 5 percent each in agriculture and in government and public works.

An old Australian saying is "Australia rides on the sheep's back." Although this saying lost force in the 20th century when manufacturing and mining expanded, more than 50 percent of the land in Australia is used for animal farming—mostly sheep and cattle. Australia remains the world's leading producer and exporter of wool and is second only to New Zealand in production of mutton (sheep meat). Australia exports more beef and veal than any other nation. More than one-sixth of the world sheep population — 140 million animals — lives in Australia, where they outnumber people by a ratio of more than 7 to 1. Thirty percent of all wool used in clothing comes from Australia. Only 10 percent of the wool produced remains in Australia; the remaining 90 percent is exported. Australia is also one of the world's largest exporters of wheat.

Almost all the world's opals, milky-white gems with translucent streaks running through them, come from Australia. Different varieties of opals have widely varying values—the striking black opals and Australian fire opals are the most sought after. Most geologists believe that Australia's opal stores have barely been tapped by mining done up to this date. Most opal mining is done in Coober Pedy, in South Australia.

Australia also has vast mineral supplies of coal reserves, iron ore, bauxite reserves, zinc, lead, nickel, and copper. Besides opals,

Australia is the world's leading producer of wool. More than one-sixth of the world's sheep live there, and they outnumber people by more than 7 to 1. Here, a flock is gathered for shearing.

Australia also has stores of other gems, including sapphires. Petroleum is extracted from the continental shelf off northwestern Australia and currently supplies more than two-thirds of domestic consumption. Scientists estimate that at present consumption rates, Australia's supplies of coal, oil, and gas will last another 100 to 300 years.

Gambling has become very big business in Australia in recent years. Sports events, such as the Melbourne Cup, bring in up to $30 million at a time. In legal gambling casinos, money is also spent with seemingly reckless abandon. It is estimated that citizens of the state of Victoria, for instance, spend $900,000 every hour on gambling. This shows once again the Australian tendency to invest heavily in leisure activities while ignoring the broader economic picture.

For the most part, Australia produces everything needed to support itself. It produces enough grains, fruits, and vegetables to feed its population and export surplus. Meat—ham, pork, beef, and lamb—is also produced in surplus for export. Televisions, radios, and telephones are manufactured there, as are just about any other products the average citizen needs. Furthermore, although consumers formerly preferred products labeled "import," today the Australians more often choose to buy products manufactured within the country.

Transportation Systems

The vast majority of Australians live in cities where urban transportation is much the same as in most other metropolitan areas throughout the world. City buses transport commuters and tourists, as do trains, streetcars, and tour buses. It is also possible to travel the length of the country by train. On short local jaunts, however, it is not unusual for riders to have to make several transfers before reaching their destination. The colonies' preferences for different rail gauges created a patchwork system that causes trouble even today. There are more than 4 automobiles for every 10 people in Australia, indicating that many Aussies prefer to drive.

In the outback, the usual means of transportation is by car (except for ranchers, who sometimes prefer horseback). Australia is served by over 500,000 miles (800,000 kilometers) of roadways. Signs

An Australian Airlines jet lands at Sydney Airport while a Qantas Airways jet waits to take off. Sydney's is the country's busiest airport, and one of the most active in the Pacific region.

along highways to the outback warn, however, that any car entering the bush should be in excellent shape and be carrying a passenger with some knowledge of mechanics. A breakdown in the outback, far from civilization, can be not only inconvenient but also very dangerous.

Air travel is the usual method of travel to and from Australia for individuals, and shipping is important for industry. Because of the continent's size, internal air transport is vital for linking the nation's far-flung cities together. In the outback, private planes and airstrips are common, and a short flight to visit a neighbor is not all that unusual. Qantas Airways (originally the Queensland and Northern Territories Air Service) and Ansett Australia provide the majority of internal commercial service, supplemented by a number of regional airlines. Qantas also offers international service to and from Australia, as do a variety of airlines from other nations. There are seven major international airports.

Communications

Radio and television broadcasts and telephone service keep Australians in touch with the world and each other. Australian broadcasting is administered by the Australian Broadcasting Commission (ABC). The commission operates a nationwide noncommercial radio and television service. The Australian Broadcasting Tribunal licenses and regulates commercial broadcasts; and the Special Broadcasting Service presents multilingual radio and television programs.

Several thousand books are published in Australia each year, but newspapers are the most popular form of reading material. More than 500 daily and weekly papers bring the news to Australians, and newspaper circulation is high. Most papers circulate only in the state in which they are published. In remote outback and rural areas, people are most interested in local news.

Only two papers are widely read nationally: the *Australian* and the *Australian Financial Review*. The three nationally popular weeklies are the *Bulletin*, the *National Times*, and the *Nation Review*. The major news agency in Australia is the Australian Associated Press. The government has recently decided to allot significant funding to the development of multimedia and computer resources. Also, the rapid expansion of the Internet during the 1990s has begun to allow isolated communities and individuals, especially in the outback, to integrate themselves easily not only into the rest of Australia but into the world at large. Over the long run, as the technology involved becomes cheaper and more accessible, this may prove one of the most important advances ever to come to Australia.

The Sydney Opera House is one of the most distinctive buildings in the world. Its completion in 1973 signaled the dawn of a new era of artistic and creative excitement in Australia.

Arts and Popular Culture

Far from being frontier dwellers in the barren outback, most Australians live in cosmopolitan cities that provide numerous opportunities for enjoying the arts. Opera, ballet, music, and theater performances of all kinds are available in Australia's major cities. Australian writers, artists, musicians, actors, and actresses have become internationally known.

The distinctive Sydney Opera House, overlooking Sydney harbor, is perhaps one of the best examples of Australian dedication to the arts. In the late 1950s, the citizens of New South Wales decided that they wanted an opera house. To find a design they loved, they held an international competition, which Danish architect Jorn Utzon won with a design that featured a series of overlapping concrete shells. Construction began in 1960. However, the opera house was not completed until 1973, and the total cost of $102 million far exceeded the original estimate of $8 million. The completed opera house rises 200 feet (60.6 meters) above Sydney harbor. This spectacular and innovative building houses operas, concerts, theater productions, and artistic exhibitions of all kinds that rival those found anywhere else in the world.

On a smaller scale, Martin Place in Sydney is a street cut off from traffic where musicians and singers perform daily, and where every Thursday the colorful ceremony of the changing of the guard at the Cenotaph War Memorial takes place. Many people feel that bustling, lively Martin Place is the true heart of the city, and tourists and natives alike wander through its length each day.

Sydney also boasts the Royal Botanic Gardens, the Rocks (the site of Sydney's first hospital, barracks, and prison, all of which have been historically preserved), Parliament House, Hyde Park, and the Sydney Harbour Bridge—one of the world's longest extension bridges. Outside Sydney, but also in New South Wales, is Australia's oldest national park—the Royal National Park, established in 1879. The park covers more than 38,000 acres (15,290 hectares) and is open for picnicking, hiking, and camping. Two other national parks are located nearby: New England National Park and Warrumbungle. A little to the north of Sydney is Hunter Valley, known for its fine wines.

Canberra, which lies within New South Wales, is the Capital Territory. The federal government administers the territory, and it is here that the day-to-day workings of the government take place. Many impressive government buildings and national museums grace Canberra. In May 1988 the new Parliament House was opened on Capitol Hill, after 8 years of construction and at a cost of $1 billion. The old Parliament House is also in Canberra and is open for tours daily. The Australian War Memorial in the capital is a tribute to Australia's role in nine wars.

The National Library of Australia is located in Canberra and houses more than 3 million items. The National Gallery and the adjoining High Court of Australia building are both the work of Australian architect Colin Madigan and are considered outstanding examples of modern architecture. The National Gallery has works by French painters Paul Cézanne and Claude Monet, by modern American artists Jackson Pollock and Andy Warhol, and fine collections of Asian and Pacific art. It also houses the world's best collection of Australian art.

Tourists come to see Government House, the residence of the governor-general, and the Prime Minister's Lodge. The Royal Australian Mint is open for tours, and visitors to the city can observe flora and fauna as well. The eastern slopes of nearby Black Mountain are the site of the National Botanic Gardens, and the Canberra Wildlife Gardens feature more than 100 species of animals and birds. Outside Canberra, the Snowy Mountains, part of the Australian Alps, attract skiers and hikers.

Melbourne, the capital of Victoria, is 400 miles (640 kilometers) southwest of Sydney. Today, residents of the two cities appear to enjoy a friendly rivalry quite different from the suspicious attitude that prevailed during colonial times. Melbourne is noted for its wide streets, lined with carefully tended, colorful gardens. The Victoria Arts Center there draws more than 12,000 visitors daily. Located on the Yarra River, the building also contains the National Gallery of Victoria. The gallery, which has a fine collection of art, is well known for its stunning stained-glass ceiling in the Great Hall and its numerous fountains. Next to the gallery is the 2,500-seat Melbourne Concert Hall, where the Melbourne Symphony Orchestra, the Victorian State Opera, and the Australian Opera perform. In the same complex are the State Theater, the Playhouse Theater, a studio auditorium, a performing arts museum, and a restaurant. The entire building is topped by a 350-foot (119-meter) tower, floodlit at night, that has become a Melbourne landmark.

Across the street from the center is the Sidney Meyer Bowl, an outdoor performance area that seats up to 100,000 people. The bowl is actually a part of the King's Domain complex, which includes the Queen Victoria Gardens, the Government House of Victoria, and the Shrine of Remembrance—a tribute to Australia's war dead.

Melbourne's Victorian Arts Center is the hub of theater, dance, and music in Victoria. The illuminated spire tops the State Theatres building, which was opened in 1984.

Besides the Queen Victoria Gardens, Melbourne also boasts its own Royal Botanic Gardens, the Royal Park, and the Royal Melbourne Zoo. There is also the Museum of Victoria, which includes a popular display of a stuffed horse named Phar Lap. Many Australians claim that Phar Lap, who raced in the late 1920s and early 1930s, was the greatest racehorse that ever lived. In 1932, he was sent to the United States for his first race there but died mysteriously before he could prove himself. The racing ability of Phar Lap was a matter of national pride to the Australians, and a few sports fans nursed a grudge toward the United States after the horse's death. Today, his body stands on display in the Museum of Victoria, and his heart, nearly twice the normal size for a horse, is preserved in Canberra's Institute of Anatomy.

Brisbane, the capital of Queensland, includes among its attractions the City Hall and its tower—once the tallest building in the area. The Lone Pine Sanctuary is famous for its koalas, and the University of Queensland contains collections of arts and antiquities. Queensland is also famous for its Gold Coast—a beautiful stretch of beach featuring luxury hotels, fine surfing, and, offshore, some of the world's best scuba and skin diving on the Great Barrier Reef.

Visitors to the Northern Territory mainly come to see the outback, wildlife, and Ayers Rock. Ayers Rock, a huge reddish sandstone boulder that rises 1,148 feet (391 meters) and stretches for 2 miles (3.2 kilometers), has long been sacred to aborigines, who call it

Brisbane, Queensland's capital, is the gateway to "the sunshine state" and the starting point for divers eager to visit the Great Barrier Reef.

Uluru. Soil cannot settle on its bare, rounded surface, and as the light and shadows change the rock seems to turn a stunning array of colors. It was returned to aborigine control in 1985 when a group of aborigines agreed to a long-term lease with the Australian government that allowed Ayers Rock to remain accessible to tourists as Uluru National Park. In addition, the Northern Territory includes Kakadu National Park— the setting for parts of the movie *Crocodile Dundee*. This park is included in the United Nations World Heritage List, a catalog of extraordinary sites all over the world that should remain unspoiled. Home to numerous aborigine groups in the past, the park has more than 1,000 sites of ancient art.

In the Alice, as the city of Alice Springs in the Northern Territory is called, visitors can tour the Old Telegraph Station—the site of the first telegraph in Australia. For the most part, although there are a number of natural attractions, the Northern Territory provides fewer opportunities for cultural pursuits than the more densely populated states.

South Australia, nicknamed the Festival State, has its own Festival Centre, including the 2,000-seat Lyric Theatre with the largest stage in all of Australia. The Festival Centre hosts musical shows, theater presentations, and many other types of cultural performances. Also located in South Australia, in Adelaide, are a number of beautiful churches. One of them is St. Peter's Cathedral, with the heaviest set of church bells in the Southern Hemisphere.

Western Australia, although isolated from the rest of the territories, still has a cosmopolitan capital city: Perth. Its economy has been helped by oil and gas discoveries in the region, and the area has a little of the feel of an isolated boomtown. Located on the southwest shore of the continent, Perth is 2,000 miles (3,200 kilometers) from Sydney. Its visitors may tour the Parliament House, walk along London Court (a mall designed in Elizabethan style and

Perth, the capital of Western Australia, has emerged as a thriving business and financial center in the wake of mineral discoveries in the state. This view is from Kingspark overlooking the city.

lined with shops), or stop by the University of Western Australia. Millionaire's Row—a suburb full of uncharacteristically large, expensive, and showy homes— is also located in Perth, as is the 8,000-seat Entertainment Centre.

The city of Hobart is the capital of the island-state of Tasmania. Its preserved and restored colonial buildings help the city retain much of its historic charm. Also located in Hobart is the Queen Victoria Art Gallery and Museum.

Aboriginal art is becoming more popular in Australia. Because many of the older examples are painted on rocks, they are not found in museums but in caves surrounding Ayers Rock and in other isolated areas, protected by the government. Aborigine paintings on

The art of the aborigines, often featuring images of animals and plants, has begun to receive recognition from art critics and collectors alike. Some designs have been used for centuries—a scene painted on a rock wall in the outback may also appear on a fashionable print dress in a Sydney boutique.

tree bark and other portable materials have become increasingly popular, and many travelers visiting Australia look for contemporary works to buy.

Several Australians have gained international reputations in the art world. George W. Lambert, Australia's first member of the Royal Academy (a prestigious group of British artists), painted during the late 19th and early 20th centuries. Among 20th-century artists, James Gleeson was known for his surrealist style, Albert Tucker for his expressionism, and aborigine painter Albert Namatjira for his desert landscapes.

Australian literature has also gained international recognition in recent years. Perhaps the most famous and beloved of all Australian writers is A. B. "Banjo" Paterson, a writer from the outback known for his novel *The Man from Snowy River* but perhaps best known for writing the definitive version of the unofficial song of Australia. The song, "Waltzing Matilda," is about a very special dancing kangaroo. Australian writer Patrick White won the Nobel Prize in literature in 1973, and Thomas Kenneally and Peter Carey have each won the prestigious Booker Prize.

Australian Entertainment

Australians have taken the entertainment industry by storm. World-renowned Australian filmmakers and movies include Gillian Armstrong (*My Brilliant Career*), Bruce Beresford (*Breaker Morant*), George Miller (*The Man from Snowy River*), and Peter Weir (*Picnic at Hanging Rock*). The "Mad Max" series of movies is popular worldwide, and the long list of Australian actors includes such notables as Merle Oberon, Errol Flynn, and Mel Gibson (although born in New York City, Gibson spent his teen and early adult years in Aus-

Bathurst Island, part of the Northern Territory, is an aborigine reserve. Considerable tracts of land have been turned over to the aborigines in recent years.

tralia). Australian-produced films such as *Strictly Ballroom* and *The Piano* have received numerous international awards in recent years.

Major pop musicians from Australia have included Olivia Newton-John, Helen Reddy, the Bee Gees, Air Supply, INXS, Midnight Oil, and the Hoodoo Gurus. For those interested in indigenous peoples, the aborigine rock band Yothu Yindi combines native concerns and sounds with a modern beat. In opera, Australia's Dame Nellie Melba became a legend, as did, later, Dame Joan Sutherland.

Actor Paul Hogan, star of the 1986 movie *Crocodile Dundee*, became a familiar face to millions around the globe when that movie,

Singer Olivia Newton-John, shown here with circus clowns, is one of many Australians who have won worldwide acclaim in the entertainment business.

about a crocodile-wrestling Aussie visiting the United States, was an instant success. Hogan also appeared in advertisements urging tourists to book passage to Australia, the fascinating land "down under" where smiling Aussies offer to "throw another shrimp on the barbie."

The barbie is Aussie slang for barbecue. Although English is the official language of Australia, Australians have adopted a somewhat hybrid version full of unique Aussie slang. The Australians, it seems, have slang terms for just about everything. *G'day* is, of course, good day. *Bloke* means man, but a bloke would not want to be called a *bludger* or a *galah*, for then he would be a scrounger and an idiot to boot. Young women are called Sheila—all of them—but Crissie is really Christmas. The bush is anywhere that is not a city or town, and a mate is a friend. Jumbucks (sheep) trot across stations (ranches). But there is one word that by itself expresses all the feelings Australians have for their country: Godzone.

Wearing traditional ceremonial paint and carrying a spear, this aborigine was among protesters during Australia's bicentennial celebration at a reenactment of the First Fleet landing.

Godzone

Australians sometimes call their country Godzone, or God's own, and in many ways this seems appropriate. The country is rich in natural resources and has an abundant supply of land for its relatively small population. In addition, it is very nearly self-sufficient in energy and produces more than enough food to feed its people. The land itself has some of the oldest and most unusual natural features in the world and is hauntingly beautiful in spots. Yet, Australia as a nation has a number of problems that it must face as it enters the 21st century.

Many of Australia's problems of recent decades have been economic, though the tide may have turned. Industry has declined somewhat as Australian manufacturing finds it difficult to compete with the high technology and low labor costs of its Asian neighbors. Though initially slow in responding to these concerns, the nation and its labor force appear to have successfully taken up the challenge.

Another very real threat to Australia's future is one that very few Australians seem to recognize. The government actively promotes tourism through its advertising campaigns, but there have been some negative effects. Economic experts point out that industry is declining, while the tourist trade is flourishing, with more resorts, golf courses, and tourist centers built each year. Fewer jobs open up

Symbols of the old and the new meet as Sydney's high-speed monorail train passes an old tavern ornamented with wood carving. Australians are proud of their position among the modern, industrialized nations, but they have learned to cherish their country's unique and colorful past.

in industry, but more and more service positions appear. Some critics claim that Australians take their easygoing attitude toward life too far and are content to enjoy the riches of the tourist trade with little thought for its far-reaching consequences. Economic advisers fear that Australia will become a nation of waiters serving wealthy Asian and American tourists drinks by the pool instead of a vital industrial power in the forefront of economic development. For a country nearly the size of the United States, this is hardly an exciting future.

Aside from the economic problems that threaten the country, some serious battles are being waged within Australia. The treatment of the aborigine population is a continuing source of dissension. On January 26, 1988, Australians celebrated the 200th anniversary of the landing of the First Fleet, commemorating the beginning of European colonization. But more than 15,000 aborigines gathered in Sydney to protest 200 years of mistreatment. Although the government has returned some land to aborigine control, past decades of prejudice and suspicion cloud the present and future of Australia's native population.

Another growing problem is substance abuse. Like most western countries, Australia is now struggling with a growing drug problem (particularly heroin). Over the past several years, the government has budgeted large sums to deal with the effects of drug abuse, but it is extremely difficult to determine the success of this campaign. Coupled with the drug problem is Australia's high rate of alcohol consumption—one of the highest in the world. Drunk-driving laws have been more strictly enforced since Australians realized that their rate of death in auto accidents was twice as high as Great Britain's and higher than that of the United States and Canada. Substance abuse must be addressed before it has a crippling effect on the country in terms of crime, health care costs, lost manpower hours, and national morale.

Still another problem facing Australia today is the welfare of future generations and the youth of today. Although education in Australia is free, young people are required to attend school only until they are 15 years of age. In Australia today, 2 out of every 3 students do not continue their education beyond age 16. The high rate of unemployment in the 16- to 20-year-old age group is certainly related to the low enrollment in higher education and does not bode well for the future of the work force.

Some Australians worry that Australia, faced with such an array of problems, may decline and fall hopelessly behind its Asian and South Pacific neighbors in the 21st century. But in view of the nation's upward rise from a desperate penal colony and the sophisticated cities rich in cultural diversity that it claims today, it is difficult to believe that Australia's future will be so bleak.

Few countries have come as far as Australia from such lowly beginnings. The problems Australia faces now are not insurmountable. Increasing international competition may be the spur to growth Australia needs. Still relatively young as a nation and buoyed by their island-continent's wealth of natural resources, Australians have many reasons to face the future with optimism.

‹GLOSSARY›

Aborigine	One of the native Australians, of whom only 160,000 are left in the country.
Boomerang	A curved weapon used by the Aborigines for hunting; some types, when thrown, will return to the thrower.
Bushrangers	Bandits who lived in the bush (many were escaped convicts), held up travelers, and ransacked isolated homes.
Dingo	Wild dog.
First Fleet	The first six ships of British convicts that arrived in Australia.
Marsupial	Derived from the Latin word for "pouch," a marsupial is a type of mammal that carries its young in a pouch. Marsupials found in Australia include kangaroos and koalas.
Outback	Land not in the cities, belonging to the bush.

◄INDEX►